The
Strictly Fish
Cookbook

The
Strictly Fish
Cookbook

by Babe and Charlie Winkelman

Published by
Babe Winkelman Productions, Inc.
Brainerd, Minnesota

Book Design	Babe Winkelman
Editor	Steve Grooms
Artwork	Duane Ryks, John Norlin, John Syverson
Research	Charlie Winkelman
Cover Design	BCW & Associates
Layout	BCW & Associates
Typesetting	Sentinel Printing
Printing	Sentinel Printing

Published by Babe Winkelman Productions, Inc.
Box 407, 213 N.W. 4th Street
Brainerd, Minnesota 56401

Printed in the United States of America

First Edition, 1985
Library of Congress Catalog
Card Number 85-52247

ISBN 0-915405-04-0

Library of Congress cataloging in
Publication Data
Winkelman, Babe & Charlie
Strictly Fish Cookbook

Brainerd, Minnesota: Babe Winkelman Productions, Inc.
ISBN 0-915405-04-0

It is with the pride and sense of accomplishment that comes from working together that both of us dedicate this book;

to all of you who care enough about nature to keep the water in your rivers, lakes and reservoirs as free of pollutants as humanly possible, ensuring that the fish we eat will remain a wonderful and healthy food;

to all of you who release alive those fish you don't plan to eat;

to our group of dedicated employees, who gave it all they had (including secret recipes), to bring this book to life;

to our daughters, Tanya, Jennifer, Jasmine and Donielle, who often give us the support we need to pursue our common and cherished career, and make our family as strong as it is;

but mostly to our Creator, for giving us the chance to go fishing.

ACKNOWLEDGEMENTS

Needless to say, we did not invent all the recipes in this book. It was from the ideas and suggestions of two special groups of people that this collection was spawned. We owe a big thanks to all our fishing friends and their families, and to all of you who use our products and contribute suggestions that help them grow and become better. We also want to say a special thank you to our group of sponsors, who have gone beyond their normal duties and even contributed recipes for inclusion here.

From many of your homes have come time-tested, family-favorite recipes. And just as important as these were the many requests we have had over the years for new ways to cook fish. It makes sense that we should add a volume on preparation, but sometimes it takes a nudge to get the creative wheels turning. By asking us for fresh methods, and by teaching us yours, you have provided exactly that.

TABLE OF CONTENTS

INTRODUCTION

One of the nicest parts of being Babe Winkelman's wife is all the fish he brings home for our family to eat.

Babe doesn't just go fishing a lot--he catches a lot of fish! Since he travels a good deal to shoot his television show, "Good Fishing," we get fish from all over--walleyes from Ontario, salmon from the Great Lakes, catfish from southern rivers, steelhead from Michigan rivers, lake trout from Manitoba, and many others.

When it comes right down to it, I think what our family likes most of all are the panfish we catch with Babe in the lakes right around our northern Minnesota home. Since we often fish with Babe for them, we get to enjoy them twice--before and after they are cooked.

As viewers of Babe's show know, he releases many of the fish he catches. Some fish he keeps just long enough for photos and then lets them go. But our whole family loves eating fish, and Babe feels good about bringing some home when it won't hurt the fish population. We don't eat rare trophy fish like muskies, for example, but we know that even if we take a few for a family dinner, most fish populations will be just as strong as before. Those meals are a natural and pleasant conclusion to a fishing trip. We also know that eating fish is healthy for us.

Since Babe catches so many fish, it just makes sense for us to use them rather than buying meat. Our family grocery bill is much lower than it would be it we had to buy those fish, or some substitute meal.

Most of all, though, our family eats fish because we love to. If fish were hard to come by, if we had to buy fish at high prices, or even if fish weren't so good for our health, I'm sure we'd still eat them for the pleasure of it! And so can you.

I won't offer tips on catching fish. That's Babe's department, and he has a series of books, audio tapes and video tapes available to help you with that. I like to fish, too, but my department is making fish taste good, and that's what this book is about.

I have full faith in these recipes. Many are standards in the Winkelman home. Others come from close friends and staff members of Babe Winkelman Productions. I've tried to avoid the difficult, overly-elaborate ones, partly because the simple recipes are so often the best ones. I hope they please you as much as they have pleased us over the years.

Charlie Winkelman

Why Eat Fish?

I've already partly answered this one by talking about how good fish can be. But let's answer it in a different way.

Every week, it seems, newspapers print stories about another scientific study that says what all the others have: what we eat has a great deal to do with our health, particularly our health in later years. Some foods are especially healthy for us and some not so healthy.

Fish is one of these especially healthy foods.

In later life, most Americans die of heart, cardiovascular diseases or cancer. Additionally, two very serious threats to the health of all Americans are obesity and excessive consumption of sodium (salt). How does fish rate as a food, then, in helping to prevent these health problems? Extremely well.

Doctors know that consumption of animal fats is unhealthy. They raise cholesterol levels and cause dangerous waxy build-ups in the circulatory system. By now we are all familiar with the classic advice from health authorities: "Eat less red meat and more poultry and, especially more fish." Eating fish, in fact, can actually reduce cholesterol levels.

The relationship between fish consumption and cancer is less clear. Recent findings do tell us, however, that eating fish (except smoked fish) is associated with noticeably low cancer rates. It is good to know that fish, unlike so many foods we like but shouldn't, is almost magically healthy.

Fish is also a highly desirable food for people who have to restrict their intake of calories (and that's most all of us!) and sodium. Fish, even saltwater fish, has very little sodium. And fish has an excellent ratio of the good stuff (protein) to the bad stuff (calories).

There's more good news. Fish provides a complete source of protein, unlike vegetables which are healthy, but incomplete sources of protein. The protein in fish is easily digested. Fish is also rich in vitamins, especially A and D, and in leaner fish, the B vitamins.

All this adds up to an overwhelming endorsement of fish as a food. It is the best, the healthiest, meat of all. We'd all be better off if we ate more fish and less of the more traditional sources of protein.

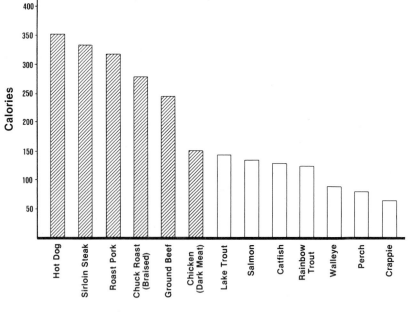

NUTRITION CHART

Meat	Calories	Protein (grams)	Fat (grams)
Chuck roast (braised)	278	22	25
Ground beef	243	20	17
Sirloin steak	328	19	27
Roast pork	317	18	25
Hot dog	351	11	21
Chicken (dark meat)	150	24	5
Fish			
Catfish	133	15	4.4
Crappie	67	14	0.7
Lake trout	145	19	9.5
Perch	77	16	0.5
Rainbow trout	132	18	5.8
Salmon	139	18	8.0
Walleye	83	17	1.3

* Adapted from research by the U.S. Department of Agriculture.

All figures are based on 3 ounce servings without sauces, oils, breading or other items that might be used; those items, of course will affect the figures.

Contaminants

As most anglers know, there is a health risk in eating some fish, from some waters.

Scientists have identified a number of chemicals that, through pollution, have entered some lakes, rivers and reservoirs. We mostly hear about polychlorinated biphenyl (PCBs), but there are others, including mercury, aldrin, chlordane, dieldrin, and most recently, dioxin. These are referred to as "persistent chemicals" because they take so long to break down in the environment.

Contaminants in the water are eaten or absorbed by plankton, which are then eaten by small fish. The contaminants can become highly concentrated in large, predatory fish (the ones we like to catch and eat) when they eat the forage fish. When we eat the contaminated predator fish, we again concentrate the chemicals to a higher degree.

These contaminants are all manmade. They have been introduced into the ecosystem recently, in biological terms, and animals have not developed a way to get rid of them. But for some reason, cold-blooded creatures like fish--even when they build up high concentrations of one of these chemicals--do not seem to develop the problems that warm-blooded animals such as humans can.

Mostly, these chemicals are worrisome because they are associated with cancer in laboratory animals. In some cases, evidence exists of developmental problems in human infants exposed to high concentration of them. Mercury has a long history of causing health problems, including mental disorders.

Most of the publicity on contaminants has centered on the trout and salmon of Lake Michigan, but many other fish and waters are now affected, including some beautiful pristine-looking Canadian waters. While there are what we might call "hotbeds" of pollution, the problem is becoming more widespread. These chemicals are now in the water system, rising in evaporating water and falling again elsewhere in rain.

So how safe are fish to eat? It depends.

It depends, somewhat, on how the fish is prepared. Two techniques will reduce contaminants in the fish. Contaminants (except mercury) attach to fatty tissue. This is concentrated in certain areas of trout and salmon and proper cleaning will remove about half of the contaminants (see the section on cleaning fish). Second, you get more contaminant- free fish if you cook it with a process that allows excess fat to drip off, such as broiling, baking or barbecuing.

Health authorities classify the degree of fish contamination based on the water the fish come from, and suggest limits on human consumption. Some fish should be avoided by everyone; some fish are fine for certain people to eat, but not others.

Women of childbearing age, pregnant or nursing mothers, and children need to restrict consumption of contaminants more than other people.

But the contaminant problem should not be exaggerated. With very few exceptions, fish are entirely safe to eat. For most of us, fish from most waters are safer to eat than just about any food imaginable. If you follow the guidelines put out by your state's health officials, you have nothing to worry about.

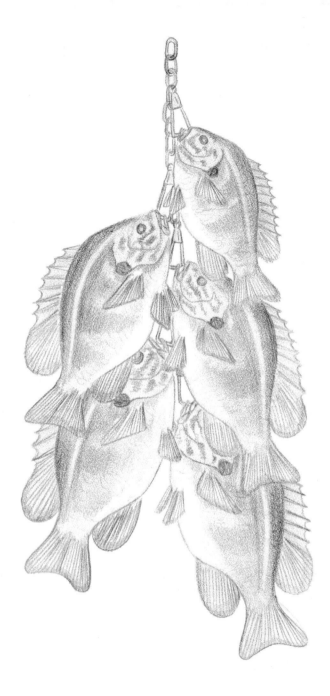

Care and Handling of Fish

It is sad to hear so many people say, "I don't care that much for fish." In many cases, I'm sure they've never really tasted fish--that is, properly handled fresh fish in all its glory.

Unfortunately, fish is more perishable than any other kind of meat. Deterioration begins shortly after a fish dies. If you don't take steps to slow it down, deterioration continues until you try to eat that fish. When many people say they don't like fish, what they actually don't like is stale, rancid, freezer burned fish.

They just don't know what a difference there is in truly fresh fish. Those same people, when they are served fish fresh out of the lake by a northwoods guide skilled at preparing shore lunches, will rave about that fish and ask for seconds and thirds.

If you take proper care of your freshly-caught fish, that wonderful "shore lunch" quality will last a long time. Give fish a chance to taste good. The results are worth it.

Care of Fish

Here are a few things to do, and not do, if you want to keep fish tasting fresh.

Don't

- Don't drag fish around for hours on a stringer in warm water. Throughout most of the year, the upper layer of water will be warm. Fish towed on a stringer will quickly die and begin to spoil. If you are fishing in very cold water, you can safely hold fish on a stringer for a short while.

- Don't leave fish on a stringer or in a livewell for a long time before cleaning them. Even fish kept in an aerated boat livewell can die if the water gets too warm.

- Don't let fish thrash around in the bottom of the boat or in your cooler or livewell. They'll bruise themselves and begin to lose quality. If you plan to keep fish, kill them with a conk on the head, just behind the eyes.

- If you kill your fish or they die, don't let them lie around in the water. Water allows harmful bacteria and enzymes to spread. That hastens the processes that spoil good flavor.

Do

- If you must kill your fish hours before cleaning them, field dress them to remove gills and entrails. These areas are the first to spoil, and they'll quickly lower the table quality of the whole fish. Thoroughly wash out the body cavity with water to remove all fluids, then chill the fish. Don't cut open the intestines or stomach; they hold powerful enzymes that will quickly destroy freshness. If you do cut these areas, wash the fish and put it on ice immediately.

- Keep fish alive and healthy, or kill them and put them on crushed ice immediately.

- Bleed your fish by cutting off the head or tail if you aren't going to fillet it right away. If fishing regulations require that the head and tail remain intact, you can cut through the tail but leave it attached by a flap of skin.

- Store fish on crushed ice whenever possible. Keep the melt water drained off. The best way is to leave the drain open and prop up the other side of the cooler. If your fish is field dressed, work some ice into the body cavity.

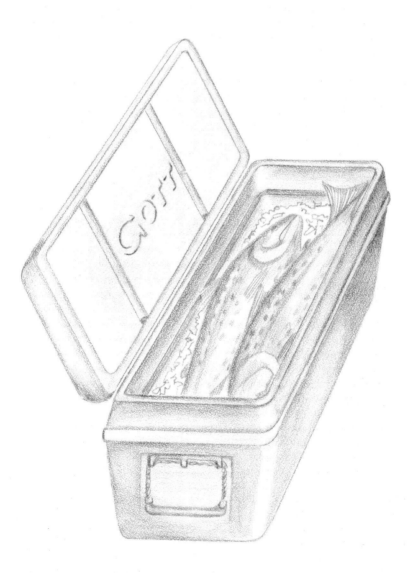

Ideal field care. In an ideal situation, you will kill your fish immediately, field dress them in the boat, rinse off all fluids, and store them in a cooler filled with crushed ice.

Can't clean them in the boat? It works almost as well to kill and ice the fish immediately. When you get off the water, field dress or completely clean the fish and get them on ice.

Can't work with crushed ice? The bags of ice you buy in vending machines will work almost as well. Try to keep the bags from breaking and spilling water into the cooler. Some anglers like to fill empty plastic milk containers with water (not to the top), freezing them, and using them as recyclable ice in coolers.

Field care without ice. The trick here is to keep the fish from lying in water or its own fluids. If you are fishing a stream for trout, use a creel that allows liquids to drain and which is ventilated to promote cooling by evaporation. Old fashioned wicker creels (still available) are better than the modern creels with plastic liners. Throw some moss or leaves under and around the fish to keep air space all around them. A wet wash cloth thrown on top will help cool the trout by evaporating slowly.

Fish can also be kept fairly cool if stored in a wet burlap bag that is kept in the shade. It also helps to pack damp moss or some other fluffy material around the fish so they aren't lying right on top and against each other, preventing air from moving around.

Field care on longer trips. Fish can be kept in excellent condition for up to a week if you super-chill them in a large cooler. In fact, fish keep better this way than if refrigerated! Here is how to super-chill your fish:

- Line the bottom of a cooler with several inches of crushed ice. Leave the drain open so melt water will not accumulate.

- Prepare a mixture of crushed ice and rock salt (ice cream salt) at a ratio of 20 parts of ice to 1 part of salt.

- Layer your skin-on, field dressed whole fish in the rock salt mixture, working ice into the body cavity. Whole, field dressed fish keep best, though you can store fillets or steaks if they are wrapped in clinging plastic wrap.

Freezing. Do not freeze fish unless you can keep them frozen until preparing them. If you are on a trip and you find it convenient to clean and freeze your fish, be sure to keep them from thawing on the way home. Frozen fillets can be stored in a cardboard box or cooler kept chilly with dry ice. Don't let the fillets come into direct contact with the dry ice, or they might get freezer burn; a layer of crumpled newspaper will insulate the frozen fillets from intensely cold dry ice.

Judging the Freshness of Fish

Let's say your fish died before you meant them to. Perhaps you found a fish that looks as if it died recently. Are these fish fresh enough to eat? How can you tell?

Fresh fish have:

- Bright eyes that often protrude.

- Red gills.

- Shiny skin, with most or all of the original color (though trout and salmon discolor very quickly, even when fresh, in a cooler).

- Flesh that springs back when pressed with a finger.

- A fresh smell, or almost no smell at all.

Stale, spoiled fish have:

- Dull, sunken eyes.

- White or grey gills.

- Dry, scaly skin that has lost its color.

- Flesh that has become so mushy that a finger pressed into it leaves a mark for a long time.

- An "off" or overly fishy smell.

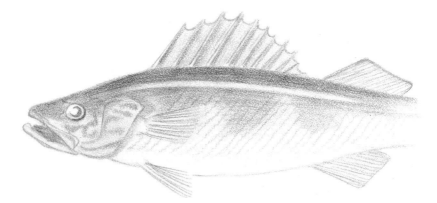

Parasites. Does your fish have visible parasites? Don't panic. These do not hurt the taste of fish or make them unfit for human consumption unless you want to eat the fish raw.

The most common parasites are the little dark flecks found on the skin of panfish, but present on walleyes or other fish. Sometimes parasites are less visible, as when they are in the flesh of fish. None of these parasites is a problem if you prepare your fish in any of the ways described in this book!

Field Dressing

The point of field dressing is to remove the sources of bacteria and the enzymes that rapidly destroy the freshness of fish. It should be done as soon as possible.

Before you begin, line the working surface with several layers of newspaper. Wipe off the fish slime with a rag or paper towel to make the fish easier to handle.

If you are going to scale a panfish before cooking it, do it now. Spoons and kitchen knives will scrape away the scales, but the inexpensive scalers sold in bait stores are better. If you are outside you won't mind the way the scales fly all over. If you are indoors, fill your sink with cold water and scale the fish below an inch or two of water; this keeps the scales from decorating your kitchen. Remove them before draining the water.

To field dress a fish:

- Cut away the lower part of the lower jaw (this will be slightly different for trout and salmon than for other fish; see illustrations).

- With larger fish, you might want to make a cut to release the gills from where they attach to the fish at the top of the throat, near the spine.

- Cut a slit from the vent to the gills, being very careful to avoid cutting the intestines or stomach. If you do, rinse off the fluids immediately in cold water.

- Grab the fish's head with one hand and the loose portion of the lower jaw assembly with the other. Pull down to free the gills and intestines.

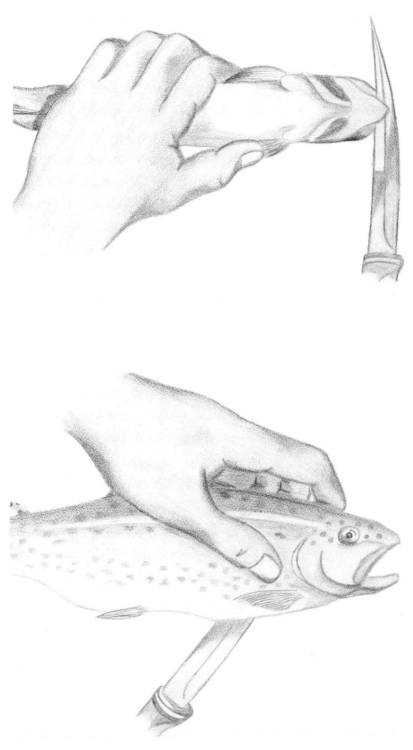

- Cut a slit through the length of the membrane near the spine that protects the kidney, or "bloodline" lying there. Remove all the dark tissue with a thumbnail or teaspoon.

- Rinse quickly in cold water.

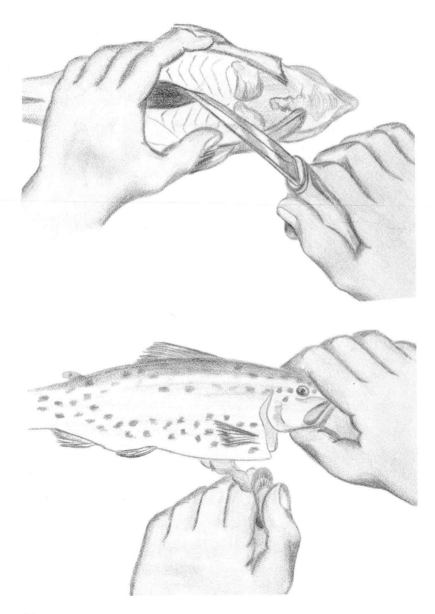

Filleting and other Cleaning Methods

It is one thing to be able to catch fish for dinner. It can be an intimidating sight, though, to look out over a mess of panfish or a stringer of walleyes that needs to be cleaned before it can be cooked.

Taken step-by-step, the process of cleaning fish can be learned fairly quickly. There are little details, however, that are important to learn.

The first thing to consider is what type of fillet knife to use. For the majority of fishermen, a regular, flexible, long-bladed knife is the best type. Some anglers clean fish with electric knives because they are fast and easy to use, and never need sharpening. The cutting effort is taken care of by the electric motor, leaving you free to guide the knife. But there are certain tasks that require a delicate touch, that an electric knife just isn't good for. And on a wilderness fishing trip, you'll need a mighty long extension cord for your electric knife.

Select a regular fillet knife with care. It should have a blade about six to seven inches long, with a tip that curves up somewhat. It is important that the blade be flexible; stiff blades will make a hash of some filleting operations, particularly the long cut that removes the skin.

Cutting through rib bones is hard on a good edge, so some fishermen like to fillet with two knives, using one with a stiffer blade for the rougher work. If you use your best fillet knife for cutting through the ribs of larger bass or walleyes, you will quickly destroy the edge and it will need to be reformed frequently with skillful use of a stone.

Sharpening knives. Dull knives make rough work of filleting. If you haven't used a truly sharp knife--and very many fishermen never have--you'll be astonished at how much easier and more pleasant the job is with one. As a bonus, you'll be less likely to cut yourself if your knife is sharp.

With experience, you will be able to put an excellent edge on a knife with a sharpening stone. But it takes experience. The key is getting a good stone and learning how to maintain the proper angle at all times while gently removing excess steel. Fillet knives are usually sharpened at an angle of 15 degrees. First, wet your stone, if your type of stone requires it. Work the blade into the stone, as if you're trying to cut a thin slice off it. Treat both sides the same, always maintaining that 15 degree angle. Start with a coarse stone and progress to a finer one. If you have a difficult time maintaining a 15 degree angle, there are devices available that lock your knife at a specific angle while you count off a number of strokes. Then, simply reverse the blade and count the same number of strokes on the other side.

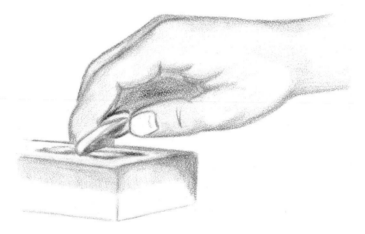

Crock sticks are easier for most people to use than a stone and are great when your knife just needs a touchup. Simply set up the sticks and stroke down with the knife held exactly up and down, first stroking down on one stick and then the other. Crock sticks come in various degrees of coarseness, but few are as coarse, or remove metal as quickly as most stones. If your blade is extremely dull, use a stone or have it professionally sharpened.

But most of your sharpening--almost all of it, in fact--should be done with a butcher's steel. You should, in fact, use the steel briefly after cleaning two or three fish.

The steel should be used after doing your rougher work with the stone or crock sticks, which take away excess metal but leave the knife edge rough.

To use a steel, point it downward while gently stroking the knife along first one side then the other. Maintain a 15 degree angle with each side.

If you treat a knife with reasonable care, a steel is all you need to keep an excellent edge. Avoid cutting through big bones, hone the blade with steel often, and you'll have a superb companion for cleaning and filleting fish.

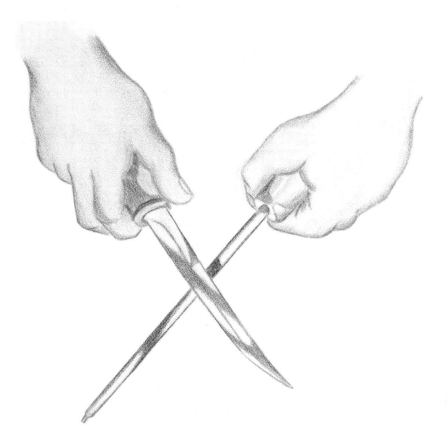

Filleting Fish

To taste best, fish should be cleaned soon after they die. It is a fact of life, though, that many of our best fishing trips are up to a week or more long, and in some cases we might not be near a good place to clean and store fish.

If you can't fillet and eat or freeze your catch right away, it should be field dressed (gutted and gilled), washed with cold water, and kept on ice. Then, it can be filleted later, or is ready for baking and similar cooking methods.

Begin your filleting by making a cut immediately behind the gills, stopping at the backbone. This cut should be angled about 45 degrees toward the head. Turn the knife toward the tail and make a long continuous cut along the backbone, cutting through the rib bones. Do not cut through the skin at the tail; leaving it attached gives you something to hold as you cut the skin off the fillet.

Flop the fillet over so the skin is down, against the newspaper. Cut the skin off the fillet by forcibly holding the knife flat to the cutting surface and then either pushing the blade along the length of the fillet, or pulling on the skin so the knife slides between the skin and meat. A little practice will teach you how to hold the knife so it cuts next to, but not through, the skin.

Do the same thing to the other side of the fish.

You now have two fillets with rib bones in them. Lay the fillets so the rib bones are up. Put the knife along the top of the rib bones, starting near the backbone, then slice the rib bones off. Keep your blade as close as possible to the bones to minimize the loss of meat. (Hint: try doing this with the fillet flopped over, rib side down; you may find this goes better.)

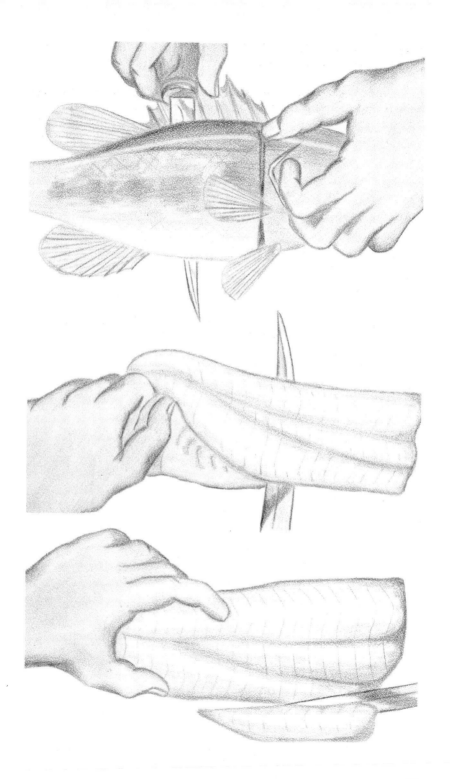

33

Alternate method. This will take a little longer at first, but will not harm the edge of a sharp knife.

Begin with the same initial cut, but instead of forcing the knife through the whole width of the fish (cutting through the rib bones), cut from the top of the fish just down to the ribs, and extend that cut toward the tail. When you get past the ribs, then press your knife through the full width of the fish cutting to the tail, as before.

Pull the meat of the fillet away from the ribs, separating it completely by gently slicing with your knife.

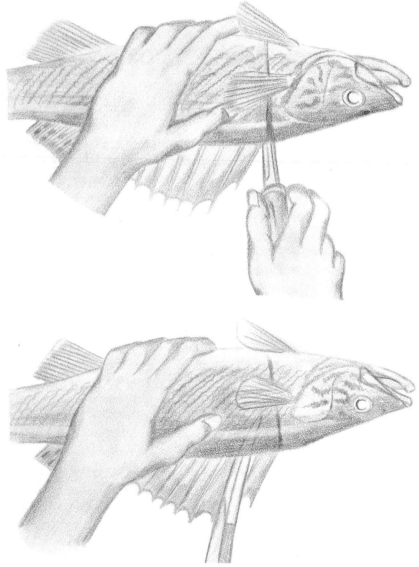

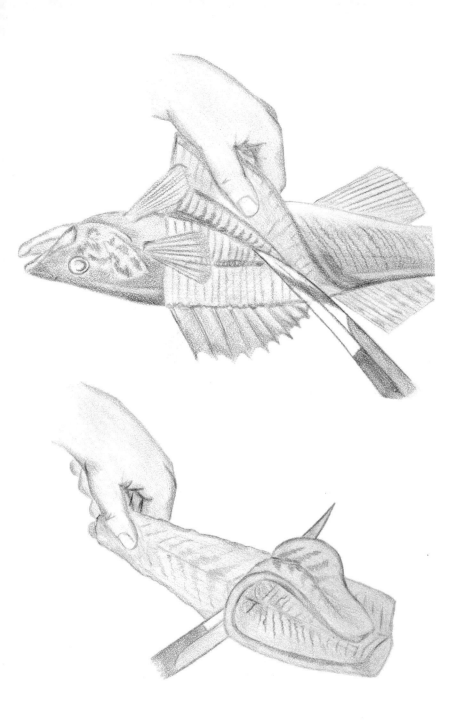

Getting Rid of the Mud Line

Some fish (especially northern pike, white bass, and largemouth bass) have a strip of dark red, grey or brownish flesh right next to the skin along the lateral line. In some cases, as with walleyes, fish from clean water will not have this distinct mud line, while fish from more polluted water will.

You should get rid of the mud line. It has an "off" taste, and this flesh quickly becomes smelly when the fish is frozen.

The strip of dark flesh, which is easily seen, can simply be sliced off with a sharp knife after the fillet is freed from the skin. An even easier solution is to aim slightly high up into the fillet with your knife when you slice the skin off the fillet, leaving the mud line on the skin.

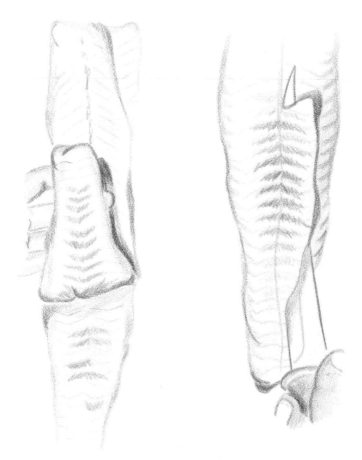

Getting Rid of Contaminants

Health officials in various states and provinces are making it easier to know whether fish might contain contaminants, by printing advisories in fishing law synopses. If you want to eat a fish from waters mentioned in those advisories, do what you can to reduce the contaminants.

Mercury, which infiltrates the flesh of fish, cannot be removed by any cleaning technique.

Fortunately, the risk can be lessened with trout and salmon by cutting out the areas of fatty tissue where contaminants concentrate. Looking at a trout or salmon in cross section, the fatty tissue will be stored in these key areas:

- at the very top of the fish, between the two muscle masses that meet above the spine;

- along the lateral line on both sides of the fish, near (though deeper than) the mud line mentioned earlier; and

- at the very bottom of the fish in the fatty belly tissue.

To reduce contaminants (by about half), these areas should be cut away. The fatty belly tissue can simply be cut, then cut V notches along the top and both sides of the fish to remove that fatty tissue.

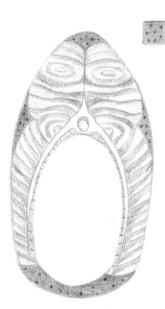

FATTY TISSUE
CONTAINING
CONTAMINANTS

Pan Dressing Panfish

Most panfish are too small to fillet. To pan dress them, scale the fish, as described before, then:

- Cut out the dorsal (top) and anal (lower back) fins by slicing your knife along each side of them, then pulling them free with pliers.

- Cut the head off at an angle, leaving as much of the thick meat in the neck area as possible. Your cut should end just behind the little pectoral fins on the lower side of the panfish. Discard the head and gills.

- Slit along the belly, avoiding the stomach and intestines, and throw away the guts. Rinse.

- Cut off and throw away the tail fin if you want, though it fries up nicely, and can be eaten.

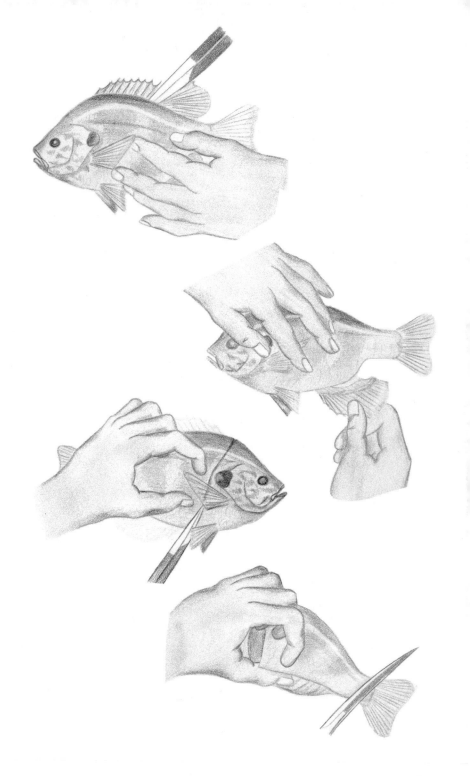

Cleaning Bullheads and Catfish

These common fish are so tasty that a number of commercial "catfish farms" have sprung up to handle the demand for them. But a great many Americans live near a wild "catfish farm"—a river, lake, or reservoir with a healthy population of catfish or bullheads. These people enjoy catching their own, and especially eating them.

Catfish and bullheads are skinned. You pull the skin off the fish with pliers, like taking off a tight-fitting glove. (Watch out for the spiny barbs; they contain a mild poison that stings for a long time.) Here's how:

- Cut a circle with a knife all the way around the fish, right behind the barbs.

- Make a shallow cut along the back to behind the dorsal fin. With bigger fish, you might also want to make a cut along the belly. These cuts give you smaller pieces of skin to work on, reducing the pressure needed to pull off the skin.

- Hold the head firmly. This is often easier if the head is fastened with a big nail driven into the filleting board or table.

- With wide-jawed pliers, pull off all the skin.

- Cut off the head from the top, using a tough knife with a thick blade. Pull the guts away with the head and discard.

- Remove the remaining fins with the pliers and cut off the tail.

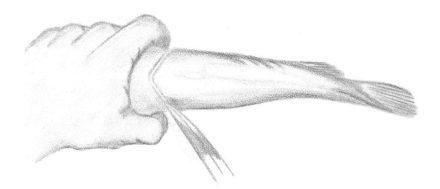

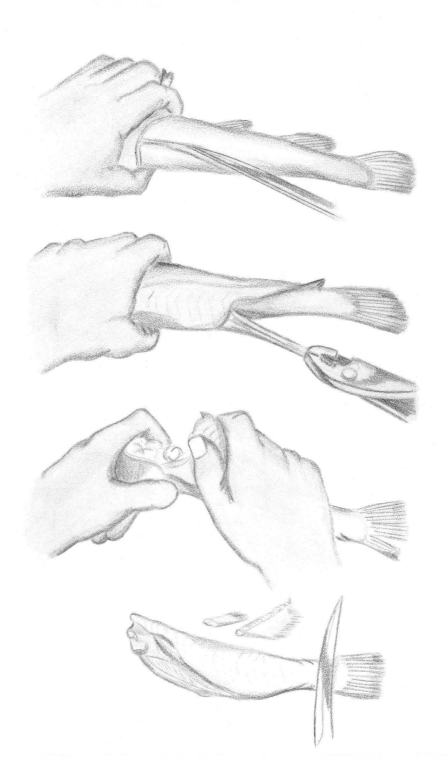

Getting Rid of Y Bones

Members of the pike family--northerns, muskies and pickerel--have Y-shaped bones in their flesh. These are a nuisance to get around while eating the fish, and fishermen have wished for generations for a way to remove them. There is a way to do it.

These bones are found in the upper half of the fillet. Their tips can be seen and felt.

With smaller fish, three pounds or less, the Y bones can be softened through cooking until they are no bother. Score the fillet with a series of knife cuts to let the heat of the oil get closer to the bones. Cook the fillets in very hot oil.

With fish over about 10 pounds, the Y bones are so large that they are easily flaked away from the cooked flesh at the table. You might not want to take the trouble to remove these Y bones, either.

With fish in the common three-to-ten pound range, it is worthwhile to cut away the Y bones.

Here's how:

- Feel where the Y bones break the surface of the fillet, just above the mid-point. Cut the fillet in two, sliding your knife just below the Y bones, going the length of the fillet. The lower portion is bone-free.
- Now you want to free the boneless top portion of the upper half of the fillet from the part that has the Y bones. Feel where the Y bones are. Slice along the top of the Y bones the whole length of the fillet. You have now freed the boneless flesh from below and above the Y bones, giving you two long, thin, and bone-free fillets.

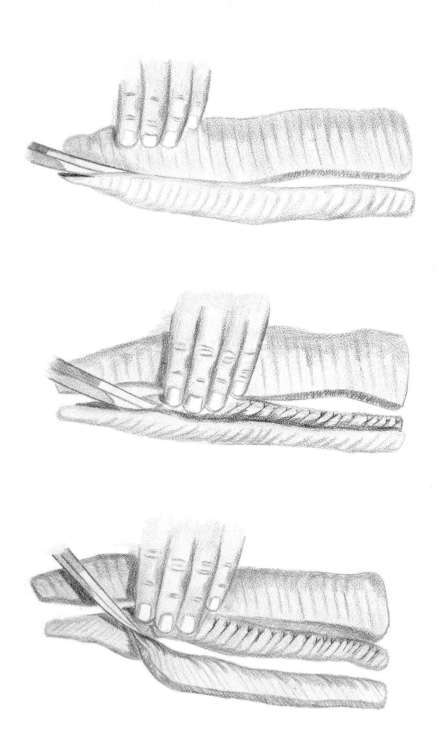

43

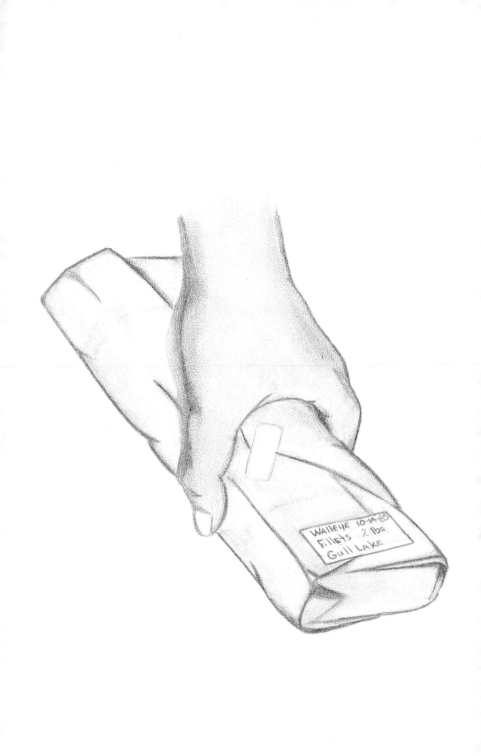

WAlleye 10-14-85
Fillets 2 lbs
Gull LAKE

Storing Fish

Perhaps the best advice about freezing fish is: don't do it unless you really have to! Freezing can't improve the quality of fish. Often it hurts it, sometimes destroying the table qualities.

If you take fish that has been abused by improper care, package it improperly, freeze it for a year or two, and then thaw it the wrong way...you have something unfit to serve the family cat! Yet this happens. No wonder so many fishermen are surprised by the wonderful taste of fresh fish at a shore lunch.

By keeping fish super-chilled, you can hold its quality for several days until you can serve it. Too often, fish frozen is fish forgotten until you discover the frosty packages at the bottom of your freezer. By then the fish is rancid or freezer burned.

Some fish do not freeze well. Grayling cooked next to a Northwest Territories river is a meal fit for a king. Fishermen who return home with frozen grayling, however, can't understand why that fish cooks up as tasteless mush at home. Grayling just can't be frozen without flavor loss. Fish with high oil content in their flesh do not survive the freezing process as well as leaner fish.

Of course, it is not often practical to serve fish within days of the time caught. Freezing, when properly done, is the best way to keep fish in top condition for the table. Start by treating the fish with care as described in the earlier chapters.

Air is the main enemy of frozen fish. Air helps carry away the moisture stored in frozen fish, causing "freezer burn." Freezer burn shows up as chalky white, leather-tough flesh that is barely edible. The second way air hurts fish is by oxidizing the polyunsaturated fats in fish flesh. Those fats, while good for us to eat, are unstable. They readily turn rancid and "off" tasting when exposed to air.

Air is the enemy. Sealing out air is the answer. Here are some general tips to help you do that:

- Clean your fish thoroughly, using water mixed with a little bit of vinegar, to remove slime.

- Fish stores longer if frozen whole or as skin-on fillets. Skinned fillets are the quickest pieces to be damaged by freezing. In general, it is smart to freeze fish whole, having chopped off heads and tails of larger fish to reduce the amount of freezer room they take up.

- Divide the fish into sensibly sized packages. If you never serve more than two people at a time, don't freeze 24 pounds of walleye fillets in one huge package.

- Be sure all packages are labeled...or you'll end up with a freezer full of "mystery meat." The label must indicate the species of fish and date packaged: "Steelhead, 5/12/ 85." It should indicate the weight of the fillets, which is easy if you have a kitchen scale; this helps you choose how much fish to thaw. The label should also indicate the way the fish was cut (filleted, steaked, whole, etc.).

- Freeze the fish as quickly as possible in the coldest part of your freezer. The freezer temperature should be 0 degrees. The coldest part is usually the lowest part of the freezer. Avoid frost-free freezer compartments of refrigerators, as the fan pulls away moisture, causing freezer burning.

- Seal the fish in plastic, foil or ice in such a way that air can't get at it and water can't leave it. Make sure there are no air pockets around the fish.

There are three recommended methods for packaging fish to be frozen.

Wrap and Freeze. Wrap the fish in materials that are impermeable to water vapor. Bad materials include: poly bags (bread wrappers), pvc freezer bags (which are not shaped properly for getting rid of air), and freezer wrap paper. Good materials include: aluminum foil (though it is easily punctured) and pvc "cling" wraps. A good procedure is to wrap the fish in two or even three layers of cling wrap, pressing out all air bubbles, then tightly wrapping freezer paper around that. The freezer paper offers a good surface for labeling.

Freezing in Ice. Put fish in containers (coffee cans with lids left off, waxed cardboard milk cartons, pvc food containers with lid left off, or simply a loaf pan or other metal pan that has the right size and shape). Cover (though, not quite fully) with water and freeze. After freezing, cap with top of coffee cans or milk containers with aluminum foil. If you used a pvc food container, now put the lid on. If you used a metal pan, run hot water to free the block of fish and ice from its mold, wrap in cling wrap or aluminum foil, and finish off with freezer paper. Label and store.

Glazing. Flash freeze the fish pieces on a pan lined with waxed paper. Dip frozen fish pieces in ice water and freeze again, keeping pieces from freezing to each other. When fish pieces have four coats of ice glazing on them, seal them in cling wrap and freezer paper. Label and store.

The Rancidity Problem

Fish flesh tends to have lots of fat in it--good fat, but fat. It turns rancid easily. The amount of fat in a fish, along with the care you take in sealing fish from air, determines how long it will keep in a freezer.

With fatty fish (see the classification to follow), you can slow down the rancidity process by freezing the fish in watered down ascorbic acid such as found in vitamin C. This process is widely used by commercial processers of frozen fruits, etc. This way you can safely keep fatty fish about twice as long as you could without the vitamin C.

Ascorbic acid (the main component of vitamin C) can be bought in drug or health stores. Mix two tablespoons of ascorbic acid in a quart of water. Dip the fish pieces in this mix for 20 seconds, then quickly freeze and wrap using one of the methods listed above.

Fat Fish - Lean Fish

It is very important to understand that not all fish are the same, and that the biggest difference is how much fat the fish flesh contains.

Understanding the fat or oil content of fish will:

- tell you how long you can store it (fatty fish cannot be stored frozen as long as lean fish);

- tell you how you should prepare fish (lean fish tastes good when cooked in oil, while fatty fish tastes best when prepared with methods that allow its natural oils to escape, such as broiling, baking, barbecuing, etc.); and

- tell you which fish can be substituted for another (you can substitute fish of similar degrees of leaness, but not a fatty fish in a recipe calling for lean fish).

Oily, fatty fish: all salmon, all trout (and char, if you want to get technical).

Moderately fatty fish: catfish (including bullheads), lake herring, suckers.

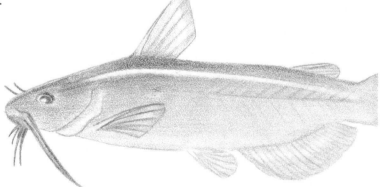

Lean fish: walleyes and perch, northern pike, muskies, pickerel, all the sunfish, all the black bass, striped bass and white bass.

Acceptable Maximum Storage times:

- Fat fish: 4 to 6 months (up to about 10 months if you use vitamin C).
- Moderately oily fish: 7 to 9 months.
- Lean fish: 9 to 12 months.

Thawing Fish

Some authorities think more fish is destroyed by harsh, overly quick thawing than any other way. Here are some tips:

- Never thaw fish at room temperature, as bacteria flourish in such an environment.

- Thaw frozen fish in your refrigerator. A one-pound package will thaw in about a day.

- Do not thaw fish in water. If you froze your fish in a coating of ice, you can run warm water over it until the ice is gone. Then thaw the fish itself slowly, in your refrigerator, in a dish covered with cling wrap.

- Keep fish wrapped in a moisture and vapor barrier while it is thawing.

- You can thaw frozen fish in a microwave. Run the microwave at half power for about four minutes a pound. Let the fish sit for several minutes, then check to see if it is thawed.

- In an emergency, you can quick-thaw frozen fish by placing it, still in its vapor barrier wrap, in a dish of cold water for two hours.

- Never re-freeze fish. Once it is thawed, use it immediately.

Cooking Technique Tips

When BAKING:
- Place fish in a greased baking dish and bake at a moderate temperature.
- Remove fish as soon as it flakes easily in the thickest portion.
- Addition of fat, oil or sauce will help keep fish moist.

When BROILING:
- Surface of fish should be 3 to 4 inches below source of heat.
- Baste fish with oil or basting sauce before and during cooking.
- Turn thicker pieces of fish halfway through the cooking time (see individual recipes).
- Do not use thin pieces or frozen fish for broiling.

There are two methods of CANNING—cold-pack and hot-pack.
- Cold-pack method: uncooked food is firmly packed into the jar and covered with boiling syrup, water, or juice.
- Hot-pack method: food is partially cooked and then loosely packed into jars that are then filled with boiling liquid.

When CHARCOAL BROILING:
- Thicker cuts of pan-dressed fish fillets and steaks are preferable.
- Grease wire grill generously to prevent fish from sticking.
- Cook fish four inches from coals.
- Baste fish with sauce or oil before and during cooking.

When DEEP-FAT FRYING:
- Do not fill fryer more than half full of oil. This will allow room for fish and bubbling oil.
- Allow fat to reach appropriate temperature (see individual recipes).
- Place only one layer of fish in the fryer. More fish may lower the temperature so fish won't brown OR cook thoroughly.
- Fry fish until it is golden brown and flakes easily.

When MICROWAVING:
You can set the oven to defrost and microwaving according to the schedule below. Only partially defrost fish. Too long will cause the outer edges to begin to cook. Remove fish from oven and let stand for five minutes. If necessary, finish thawing fish under cold running water.

Fish	Weight	Defrosting Time in Microwave
frozen fillets	1 lb. pkg.	3 min; turn over; 3- 4 minutes
whole fish	1 1/2-1 3/4 lb.	5 min; turn over; 5-6 minutes
steaks	1 lb.	4-5 minutes

Make sure fish is completely defrosted before starting to cook it. If it is not, you may find ice crystals in the center of the fish after cooking.

OVEN FRYING is a hot oven method which simulates pan frying.
● Place breaded fish in a well-greased baking pan.
● Pour oil or melted fat over fish and bake at 500 degrees F. until fish flakes easily.
● Fish need not be turned or basted.

PAN FRYING is cooking in a small amount of fat or oil.
● Choose a fat or oil that can be heated to a high temperature without smoking such as vegetable oil.
● Place a single layer of fish in about 1/8 inch hot fat or oil.
● Fry fish until lightly browned.
● Turn and lightly brown the other side.

POACHING is cooking in a simmering liquid.
● Place a single layer of fish in a large shallow pan, such as a frying pan.
● Barely cover fish with liquid. The liquid may be lightly salted water, milk, a mixture of white wine and water or seasoned water.
● Simmer in covered pan until fish flakes.

When cooking fish in a WOK:
● All fish and any accompanying vegetables should be cut small into small pieces and cooked in order with the things that take longest started first (i.e. carrots), so everything is done at the same time.
● Use a small amount of oil. Generally, 1—2 tablespoons is enough to cook the whole meal.

BAKING

Baked Bass in Tomato Sauce

2 bass	4 strips bacon
1 can cream of tomato soup	1/4 tsp. salt
1 cup celery, chopped	1/8 tsp. pepper

Preheat oven to 350 degrees. Salt and pepper bass inside and out. Stuff cavity with celery. Sew up opening and score fish in several places. Place in a baking dish, add a small amount of water. Lay bacon strips over fish and bake for about 1 1/2 hours or until fish is done. Remove fish from pan. Add tomato soup to remaining liquid and blend well. Bring to a full boil and pour over fish.

Baked Bass in White Wine

1 1/2—2 lbs. striper fillets	1 bay leaf, broken into pieces
1 Tbsp. cooking oil	1 Tbsp. parsley, minced
1 onion, chopped	salt and pepper
1 can (14 1/2 oz.) tomatoes	1/4 cup bread crumbs
1/4 cup dry white wine	1 lemon, cut into wedges

Preheat oven to 400 degrees. Cut fillets into serving pieces and lay in a buttered casserole. Cook the onion in oil in a skillet over medium heat for 7 minutes. Add tomatoes, wine, bay leaf, parsley, and a little salt and pepper. Cook over high heat for 10—15 minutes until the liquid is reduced and the flavors are blended. Pour the sauce over the fillets and sprinkle with bread crumbs. Bake in oven for 25—30 minutes, until fish flakes easily with fork. Serve with lemon wedges.

Baked Carp and Vegetables

4 lbs. carp	2 tomatoes, chopped
1 green pepper, chopped	1/2 cup cooking oil
1/4 cup celery, diced	salt and pepper
1 carrot, diced	flour
1 onion, diced	paprika

Preheat oven to 375 degrees. Combine vegetables and place in baking dish with oil. Season carp (either whole or sliced) with salt and pepper, then roll in flour and place on vegetables; sprinkle with paprika. Bake for 40 minutes or until browned, basting frequently.

Baked Carp with Cheese

2 cups cooked carp, flaked	1 can cream of mushroom soup
1 cup onion	1/2 tsp. salt
2/3 cup green pepper, diced	paprika
2 cups celery, diced	nutmeg
1/2 cup mushrooms (fresh or canned) cut into small pieces	1 tsp. lemon juice
	1/2 cup buttered crumbs
	1/2 cup Swiss cheese, grated
2 Tbsp. butter	

Preheat oven to 350 degrees. Cook onion, green pepper, celery, and mushrooms in 2 tablespoons butter until tender. Pour in soup, add seasonings and lemon juice. Mix. Add fish, mix gently. Pour into buttered 1 1/2 quart baking dish and cover with buttered crumbs and cheese. Bake in oven 25—30 minutes or until golden brown.

Baked Catfish

4 lbs. catfish fillets	1/2 tsp. marjoram
5 Tbsp. butter	2 cans condensed milk
1/2 tsp. dry mustard	3/4 cup flour
1/4 tsp. tarragon	

Preheat oven to 325 degrees. Melt butter in baking dish. Mix flour, mustard, marjoram and tarragon. Dip catfish in milk, then roll in flour mixture. Place in melted butter and bake for 20 minutes. Remove from oven, turn and bake for another 15 minutes. Serve with tartar sauce. Serves 3 to 4.

Baked Coho with Dressing

1 large coho (10—12 lbs.)
salt and pepper
lemon
paprika

1/2 package of prepared bread
  dressing or stuffing
4 slices bacon chopped
1 onion, chopped
1 cup celery, chopped

Preheat oven to 350 degrees. Clean fish well. Rub cavity with butter and lemon juice. Season with salt, pepper and paprika. Cook bacon. saute onion and celery in bacon. Follow directions on package for dressing. Add more water, if necessary, to make dressing moist. Add onion, bacon and celery to dressing. Fill cavity and close with skewers or tie with string. Rub outside of fish with butter and lemon juice, and season with salt, pepper and paprika. Bake 20 minutes per pound or until fish flakes with a fork. Baste with lemon butter.

Baked Coho with Sour Cream Stuffing

3—4 lbs. dressed coho
1 1/2 tsp. salt

Sour Cream Stuffing
2 Tbsp. melted butter or
   margarine

Sour Cream Stuffing:

3/4 cup celery, chopped
1/2 cup onion, chopped
1/4 cup melted butter
1 qt. toasted bread crumbs or
   herb seasoned croutons

1/2 cup sour cream
1/4 cup peeled lemon, diced
2 Tbsp. grated lemon rind
1 tsp. salt
1 tsp. paprika

Preheat oven to 350 degrees. Clean, wash and dry fish. Sprinkle cavity with salt. Stuff fish loosely and close with skewers or with string. Place in a well greased shallow baking pan. Brush with melted butter and bake in oven for 45—60 minutes or until fish flakes easily with a fork. Baste occasionally with melted butter.

Baked Creamed Fish

1 (4—6 lb.) lean fish
1/2 tsp. salt per lb. fish
pepper
flour

3 Tbsp. onion, chopped
1/4 cup butter
2 cups heavy cream

Preheat oven to 350 degrees. Wash fish thoroughly; pat dry with paper towels. Season with salt and pepper and roll in flour until completely coated. Sprinkle chopped onion inside fish. Melt butter in skillet and brown fish on all sides. Place fish in a shallow baking pan; pour cream over fish. Bake for 1 1/2 hours, basting every 30 minutes. Garnish with parsley.

Baked Eel With Gravy

4 lbs. eel
1/2 cup flour

2 Tbsp. butter

Preheat oven to 350 degrees. Coat each piece with flour. Place in baking pan with small amount of salted water. Add a few dabs of butter and bake for 30 minutes. Remove eels from pan and make a gravy (in same pan) with a little butter, flour and water. Bring to a boil and pour over eel. Serve.

Baked Fillets in Dill Sauce

1 1/2 lbs panfish fillets
1 tsp. salt
1/4 tsp. pepper
1/3 cup flour

1 1/2 cups dill sauce
2 Tbsp. chives or green onion
  tops, chopped

Preheat oven to 350 degrees. Sprinkle fish with salt and pepper and roll in flour. Place in a single layer in a greased shallow casserole. Completely cover with dill sauce. Bake for 15—20 minutes or until fish flakes. Garnish with chives.

Baked Fish

1 (2—3 lb.) bass, filleted
1 stick butter, melted
1 tsp. garlic powder
1 tsp. Worcestershire sauce

pinch of thyme
pinch of marjoram
salt and pepper

Preheat oven to 250 degrees. Cover bottom of roasting pan with foil. Rinse fish; salt and pepper generously. Place in roasting pan. Melt butter in small saucepan, add Worcestershire sauce and seasonings. Pour over fillets. Place in refrigerator and let stand 1 hour. Bake, covered, for at least 45 minutes, until fish are brown and crisp.

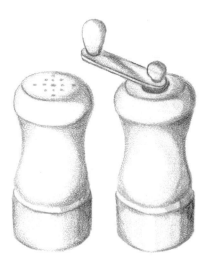

Baked Fish Au Gratin

2 cups cooked fish
1 Tbsp. green pepper, chopped
3 Tbsp. butter
3 Tbsp. flour

1/4 tsp. paprika
2 cups milk
1 cup buttered bread crumbs

Preheat oven to 350 degrees. Saute onion and green pepper in 3 tablespoons butter until tender. Mix in flour and paprika then gradually add milk. Heat to boiling. Place fish in greased baking dish, pour milk-flour mixture over and cover with crumbs. Bake for 20 minutes or until crumbs are browned.

Baked Fish Fillets

1 lb. fish fillets
1 Tbsp. onion, minced
4 Tbsp. butter
1/2 tsp. salt
dash pepper

1 1/2 cups soft bread crumbs
1/4 cups American cheese
   grated
1/2 cup milk

Preheat oven to 350 degrees. Cut fish into serving-size pieces and place into shallow baking dish. Saute the onion in butter. Sprinkle with salt and pepper, add bread crumbs and cheese and toss until well mixed. Spread over fillets and press down firmly. Pour milk around the fish and bake in oven for about 45 minutes.

Baked Fish-Wich

1 1/2 lbs. fish fillets
salt and pepper
1 cup milk
2 Tbsp. prepared mustard
paprika

8 slices bread
2 eggs
1/4 cup mayonnaise
6 slices processed American
   cheese

Preheat oven to 325 degrees. Arrange half the bread in a greased, shallow baking dish. Place fish on bread; season with salt and pepper. Top with remaining bread. Beat eggs, milk, mayonnaise and mustard together; pour over bread. Arrange cheese on top and sprinkle with paprika. Bake for 40 to 45 minutes until a knife inserted in the center comes out clean.

Baked Fish with Potatoes and Eggs

1 1/2—2 lbs. fish fillets
(flounder, bass, any lean
unoily fish you like)
3 large potatoes, peeled and cut
cut into 1/2 inch slices
1 large onion, minced
2 Tbsp. butter

1/4 tsp. salt
1 cup milk
1 Tbsp. cornstarch
1/4 cup grated cheese
4 hard cooked eggs, sliced
1/4 tsp. cayenne pepper

Preheat oven to 350 degrees. Butter or oil a baking dish and put in a layer of potato slices. Saute onion in melted butter in a large pan. Add a layer of fish fillets to the baking dish and sprinkle with the sauteed onion, and salt. Alternate layers of potatoes and fish, ending with potatoes as the top layer.

Stir milk into cornstarch in a small bowl. In a small sauce pan over low heat combine cornstarch mixture and cheese. Bring it slowly just to the boiling point, until thickened. Pour the milk mixture over the layers of potatoes, fish and onions in baking dish. Arrange the slices of hard cooked eggs over the potatoes and sprinkle with cayenne pepper. Bake covered for 30 minutes.

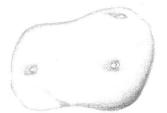

Baked Fish with Tomato Sauce

1 lb. fish fillets
1 cup onion, chopped
2 Tbsp. butter
1 Tbsp. flour

1 can consomm'e, undiluted
1/2 cup catsup
3/4 cup sliced dill pickle

Preheat oven to 400 degrees. Saute onions in butter. Stir in flour and gradually add consomm'e and catsup. Simmer 25 minutes, stirring occasionally. Add pickles. Place fish in shallow baking dish and cover with sauce. Bake in oven for 25 to 30 minutes or until fish flakes easily with a fork.

Baked Haddock in Cream

1 1/2 lbs. haddock fillets
2 Tbsp. lemon juice
1 tsp. prepared mustard
1/2 tsp. Worcestershire sauce
1 tsp. salt

1/4 tsp. pepper
3 small onions, sliced
1 cup cream
parsley
paprika

Preheat oven to 400 degrees. Wipe haddock with damp cloth and place in baking dish. Mix lemon juice, mustard, Worcestershire sauce, salt and pepper together and pour over haddock. Add onions and cream. Bake about 30 minutes. Sprinkle with paprika and garnish with parsley.

Baked Halibut Au Gratin

2 lbs. halibut steaks
1 1/2 tsp. salt
1/4 tsp. pepper
1/4 cup flour
2 Tbsp. onion, grated

1 can (10 1/2 oz.) cream of
    mushroom soup
1 cup cheese, grated
2 Tbsp. parsley, chopped
paprika

Preheat oven to 350 degrees. Combine salt, pepper and flour. Roll fish in flour mixture and arrange in single layer in well greased shallow baking dish. Heat mushroom soup (undiluted) in saucepan until smooth. Pour over fish. Top with grated cheese and parsley. Sprinkle with paprika. Bake for about 30 minutes, until fish flakes easily with a fork.

Baked Lake Trout

2—4 lbs. lake trout
1/4 tsp. oregano
1/4 tsp. celery salt
1/4 tsp. basil

1/4 tsp. paprika
1/4 cup lemon juice
1/4 cup melted butter

Preheat oven to 350 degrees. Combine all ingredients except fish. Place fish in greased baking dish and baste with butter mixture. Bake approximately 20 minutes.

Baked Lake Trout Fillet

1 large trout, filleted
1 large onion, sliced
1 tomato, sliced
1 large potato, sliced

1 Tbsp. mayonnaise
salt, pepper and paprika
melted butter
3 slices of green pepper

Preheat oven to 350 degrees. Place one fillet on a large piece of aluminum foil. Season with salt, pepper and paprika, then spread with mayonnaise. Layer sliced potatoes, onion, tomatoes and green pepper on fillet. Place second fillet (which has been seasoned with salt, pepper and paprika) on top of layered vegetables. Tie with cord, or use skewers, to hold fillets together. Wrap with foil and seal tightly. Place on baking sheet and bake for 1 hour or until fish flakes with a fork.

Baked Northern in Dill Sauce

4 northern fillets
  (about 1/2 lb. each)
1 can stewed tomatoes

1 cups onions, chopped
3/4 Tbsp. dill seed

Preheat oven to 400 degrees. Place fillets in a baking dish. Mix tomatoes, onion and dill seed together and pour over fish. Bake for about 30 minutes.

Baked Perch

3 lbs. perch fillets
1 Tbsp. flour
1 1/2 Tbsp. butter
1 bay leaf
1 onion, minced

salt and pepper
1 chicken bouillon cube
1 cup hot water
1/2 cup bread crumbs
1 tsp. lemon juice

Preheat oven to 400 degrees. Spread perch fillets evenly in a greased baking dish. Melt butter in a small pan. Stir in flour and onions. Dissolve bouillon cube in 1 cup hot water and add flour mixture then add bay leaf. Stir and simmer for 15 minutes, until mixture is thickened. Add lemon juice, salt and pepper. Remove bay leaf and continue stirring. Pour over fillets and sprinkle with bread crumbs. Bake for 20 minutes.

Baked Perch Fillets

8 medium sized perch fillets
1/4 cup parsley, finely chopped
2 Tbsp. parsley, finely chopped

2 Tbsp. fresh dill, chopped
  or 1 tsp. dill seed
1/4 cup hot water

Preheat oven to 350 degrees. Cover bottom of baking dish with 1/4 cup parsley, arrange fish over this. Sprinkle with remaining parsley, fresh dill or dill seed and add hot water. Bake for 20 to 25 minutes.

Baked Salmon Loaf

1 lb. salmon, flaked
2 cups bread crumbs
1 cup milk, warmed
1/2 tsp. salt

6 eggs, yolks and whites
  beaten in separate bowls
1 Tbsp. butter

Preheat oven to 350 degrees. Combine the bread crumbs with the warm milk in a sauce pan. Stir and beat with fork until smooth, away from heat. Combine fish with the crumb-milk mixture. Add salt and combine mixture with the egg yolks, and then fold in whites. Put mixture in a buttered casserole, set it in a pan holding 2 inches of hot water and bake for 30 minutes.

Baked Salmon Steaks in Egg-Lemon Sauce

2 lbs. salmon steaks
2 Tbsp. butter
1/4 lb. fresh or canned
  mushrooms, chopped
1/2 tsp. salt
1/4 tsp. pepper

1 cup milk
2 eggs, beaten
2—3 Tbsp. lemon juice
parsley sprigs, tomato slices,
  small red radishes as
  garnishes

Preheat oven to 350 degrees. Melt butter in large pan, over medium heat. Add mushrooms and cook, stirring until they are tender.

Butter a large baking dish. Sprinkle the fish with salt and pepper. Put cooked mushrooms into baking dish, place fish steaks on top, side- by-side.

Pour the milk in a bowl, beat in the beaten eggs and lemon juice. Pour mixture over the fish steaks. Bake until a fork goes through the fish quite easily, approximately 30 minutes. Arrange fish on a heated platter, surrounded with parsley sprigs, tomato slices and radishes.

Baked Stuffed Carp

3 lbs. carp, dressed for
  baking
3 Tbsp. onion, finely chopped
4 slices bacon
1 tsp. sage

4 cups bread crumbs
3/4 cup celery, finely cut
6 Tbsp. butter, melted
1/8 tsp. pepper

Preheat oven to 375 degrees. Cook celery and onion in butter. Mix other ingredients and add to butter mixture. Dampen fish and salt lightly inside and out. Stuff with dressing and sew or tie with string. Bake for 1 hour.

Baked Stuffed Fish with Rice

4 small fish, about 1/2 lb. ea.
  after head and tails are removed
2 Tbsp. onions, chopped
1/2 tsp. salt

1 Tbsp. oil
2 cups cooked brown rice
1/4 tsp. pepper
1/8 tsp. dill

Preheat oven to 350 degrees. Wash fish and pat dry with paper towels. Saute the onions and dill in oil until tender, but not brown. Combine with rice and mix well. Season to taste. Put 1/2 cup of stuffing in each fish cavity and place in greased, shallow baking pan; brush fish lightly with oil and bake in oven for 20 minutes.

Baked Trout

4—6 medium-sized trout
  (about 1/2 lb. each)
juice from 1 lemon
1 tsp. salt
1 clove garlic, minced

1 cup white wine
2 Tbsp. parsley, chopped
2 Tbsp. green onion, chopped
2 Tbsp. dry bread crumbs
4 Tbsp. melted butter

Preheat oven to 400 degrees. Wash trout thoroughly and dry with paper towels. Rub outside with lemon juice and sprinkle with salt. Arrange minced garlic in bottom of a buttered, shallow baking pan. Place fish in a single layer over garlic and pour wine over top. Sprinkle with parsley, green onions and dry bread crumbs, then spoon on butter. Bake for 20 minutes.

Baked Trout, Bass or Pike

1 whole fish
2 cups bread crumbs
milk
1 egg
3 slices bacon, chopped fine
3 slices uncooked bacon

salt and pepper
nutmeg
thyme
1/2 cup hot water
lemon wedges
1 Tbsp. butter
1 Tbsp. flour

Preheat oven to 350 degrees. Clean fish, wash thoroughly and dry. To make dressing: Wet bread crumbs with milk, add egg, chopped bacon, salt, pepper, nutmeg, and thyme. Mix well. Stuff fish cavity and truss. Fry 3 pieces of bacon until brown. Place bacon into the pan the fish is to be baked in and add 1/2 cup of hot water. Place the fish in the pan, dot with butter, sprinkle with salt and bread crumbs. Bake, basting often, until fish flakes easily with a fork. Place fish on a serving platter. In a separate pan, melt butter, add flour. Add a little more water. Pour stock into baking pan; bring to a boil, then pour over fish. Garnish with lemon wedges.

Baked Trout Fillets

12 trout fillets
1 egg
1/3 cup evaporated milk
salt and pepper
1 cup crushed cracker crumbs

1/2 cup butter
12 small slices cheddar cheese
3 fresh tomatoes, sliced
juice from 1 lemon

Preheat oven to 350 degrees. Beat egg, add milk and seasoning. Dip fillets in egg mixture then in cracker crumbs. Melt butter in skillet and brown fillets. Remove from skillet and place on a cooking sheet. Sprinkle with lemon juice and top each fillet with a slice of tomato and cheese. Bake for about 25 minutes.

Baked Trout with Sour Cream

5 lbs. lake trout
2 cups sour cream
1/4 cup melted butter

2 Tbsp. chopped parsley
1 tsp. paprika

Preheat oven to 400 degrees. Split and remove bones from lake trout. Rub fish, inside and out, with paprika and butter. Place in large baking dish and cover with sour cream. Sprinkle with parsley. Cover and bake for 45 minutes.

Baked Trout with Tomatoes

3 1/2 lb. trout
salt
2 1/2 cups cooked tomatoes
1/4 cup onion diced
1/2 tsp. Worcestershire sauce

1/2 cup celery, diced
1 egg yolk
1/2 cup cream
juice from cooked tomatoes

Preheat oven to 350 degrees. Rub trout with salt. Place in a baking pan. Cook tomatoes, drain, this will be your juice. Cover with tomatoes, onion and celery. Bake 40 to 45 minutes, until fish flakes with fork. When trout is done, place on a hot platter and keep warm while preparing sauce.

Strain tomato juice. Beat egg yolk with cream, add tomato juice and Worcestershire sauce. Heat to boiling and cook for 2 minutes. Pour over fish and serve.

Baked Walleye

1 (3—4 lb.) walleye, dressed
5 strips of bacon
1 onion, sliced
1 lemon, thinly sliced
1 can (medium size) plum
   tomatoes, peeled, reserve juice from tomatoes

1 clove garlic, minced
1/2 tsp. salt
1/8 tsp. pepper
2 Tbsp. water
dash of cayenne pepper

Preheat oven to 400 degrees. Rub fish with salt and pepper and lay in a roaster on bacon strips. Add water, cover and simmer for 10 minutes.

Saute garlic, onion and tomatoes in butter, add cayenne pepper and tomato juice. Bring to a boil and pour over fish. Reduce heat to 325 degrees. Cover the fish with lemon slices and cook, uncovered, 45 minutes.

Baked Walleye in Sour Cream

1 1/2 lbs. walleye fillets,
   cut into bite size pieces
1 cup sour cream
1 Tbsp. flour
1/2 cup dry white wine

2 Tbsp. finely chopped green
   onions
1/2 tsp. parsley
salt and pepper to taste
1 small jar pimento, chopped

Preheat oven to 325 degrees. Place fillets in a lightly greased baking dish. Mix all other ingredients, except pimento, and pour over fillets. Bake for about 25 minutes. Sprinkle pimento pieces over top and bake for another 5—10 minutes.

Baked Walleye with Vegetable Dressing

3—4 lbs. walleye fillets
1/4 cup green pepper, chopped
1/4 cup butter
3/4 cup shredded carrots
1 1/2 Tbsp. lemon juice
1 egg, beaten
1/4 tsp. pepper

1 onion, chopped
1/4 cup celery, chopped
1/2 cup mushrooms, chopped
2 3/4 cups dry bread crumbs
1 Tbsp. snipped parsley
1 1/2 tsp. salt

Preheat oven to 350 degrees. Soak fillets a few minutes in salted water. Saute onion, green pepper, celery, mushrooms and carrots. Remove from heat add to bread crumbs. Lightly mix add parsley and egg, add a little chicken broth if too dry. Drain fillets. Lay fillets on buttered foil in large pan. Pat dressing on top and cover with remaining fillets. Sprinkle with salt, pepper and paprika. Baste with lemon juice and butter. Cover with foil and bake until fish is tender, basting occasionally.

Baked Whitefish in Almond Sauce

1 whitefish (2—3 lbs.)
4 Tbsp. butter
1 1/2 pints basic cream sauce
paprika

1/4 tsp. almond extract
2 oz. slivered almonds
yellow food coloring

Preheat oven to 350 degrees. Melt butter in a large heavy skillet and brown fish. Place fish in a deep baking dish. Add a few drops of yellow food coloring, almond extract, and slivered almonds to basic cream sauce. Mix well. Cover fish with sauce. Bake in covered dish for about 1 hour. Remove and sprinkle with paprika.

Barbecued Fish

Preheat oven to 350 degrees. Season fish fillets with salt and pepper. Place in baking dish. Make a sauce of:

3 Tbsp. fat
2 Tbsp. onion, minced
2 Tbsp. vinegar
salt and pepper

1 small clove garlic,
  sliced
2 Tbsp. brown sugar
2/3 cup catsup

Lightly brown onion and garlic in fat. Add the rest of the ingredients and heat well. Pour over fish and bake for 30 minutes or until fish is done.

Basil Perch

1 lb. perch fillets
1 can (4 oz.) tomato paste
1 small zucchini, sliced
1 can (8 oz.) corn
1 small onion, thinly sliced

2 oz. Parmesan cheese
salt and pepper
basil to taste
1 lemon, cut in wedges

Preheat oven to 350 degrees. Combine in a baking dish all the vegetables. Mix in the tomato paste and seasonings and top with cheese. Bake for 20 minutes. While vegetables are cooking, melt butter and add lemon juice.

Saute fillets in lemon butter until flakey. Top with vegetable mixture. Sprinkle with Parmesan cheese and freshly-squeezed lemon.

Bass in Onion Soup

2 large bass fillets	1 pkg. prepared onion
(approximately 2 lbs.)	soup mix
salt and pepper to taste	1 cup white wine
garlic powder	paprika

Preheat oven to 350 degrees. Wash fillets and dry with paper towels. Place on a large piece of aluminum foil. Season with salt, pepper, and garlic powder. Turn up edges of foil as if to make a bowl. Pour in the wine and add the package of onion soup mix, and sprinkle with paprika. Seal tightly and wrap in additional foil. Bake for 1 1/2—2 hours or until fish flakes with fork.

Bass in Wine

6 bass fillets (6—9 oz. ea.)	salt and pepper
1 tsp. tarragon	1 Tbsp. butter, melted
1/4 cup white wine	1 Tbsp. Worcestershire sauce
2 Tbsp. onion, diced	chives, chopped

Preheat oven to 350 degrees. Soak tarragon in white wine for 20 minutes. Place bass fillets in buttered casserole, sprinkle with diced onion. Dot with butter, season with salt and pepper, add wine. Cover casserole with buttered wax paper. Bake for 10 minutes. Remove wax paper, add melted butter, sprinkle with Worcestershire sauce. Replace paper; bake another 15 minutes. Remove wax paper for the last 5 minutes. Sprinkle with chopped chives. Serve.

Bass Parmesan

2 lbs. bass fillets	1/2 tsp. lemon juice
1/4 cup butter, melted	2 Tbsp. white wine
1/2 tsp. salt	4 Tbsp. grated Parmesan cheese
1/4 tsp. pepper	1/2 tsp. paprika

Preheat oven to 425 degrees. Pour small amount of butter in shallow baking pan to cover bottom. Place fillets in a single layer, skin side up; salt and pepper. Bake for 15 minutes. Turn fillets, add lemon juice and white wine, sprinkle with Parmesan cheese and paprika. Bake another 5 minutes or until fish flakes.

Bass Puffs

1 cup cooked, flaked bass
1 cup mashed potatoes
1/2 cup milk

2 eggs
1/2 tsp. paprika
salt and pepper to taste

Preheat oven to 350 degrees. Mix flaked bass, milk, salt, pepper, paprika, and one egg in a mixing bowl. Place in greased casserole dish and bake for 20 minutes. Beat remaining egg white until stiff. Stir in yolk and spread mixture over bass. Return to oven until top is golden.

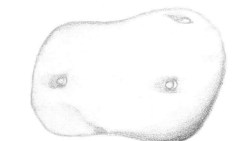

Bass with Anchovy-Caper Butter

5—6 bass fillets
1 Tbsp. capers, mashed
1 green onion, minced
2 Tbsp. anchovy sauce

4 Tbsp. butter
2 cups bread crumbs
1/4 cup dry white wine
2 springs parsley, minced

Preheat oven to 375 degrees. Mix capers, onion and anchovy sauce with butter. Spread on fillets, roll in bread crumbs and place in buttered baking dish. Add wine and bake for 20 minutes. Sprinkle with parsley.

Brook Trout Vino

6 brook trout
1 cup water
1 1/2 cups dry wine

2 Tbsp. Worcestershire sauce
1 cup melted butter
salt and pepper

Preheat oven to 350 degrees. Cover the bottom of a small roasting pan with butter. Mix wine, water, salt, pepper and Worcestershire sauce. Place trout in roasting pan, pour butter evenly and generously over fish. Pour wine mixture over fish. Bake for 40—45 minutes.

Carp Casserole

2 cups cooked carp, flaked
2 cups cooked rice
3/4 cup onion, chopped
1/4 cup green pepper, diced

2 Tbsp. butter
1 can cream of celery soup
1/2 cup milk
3/4 cup bread or cracker crumbs

Preheat oven to 350 degrees. Saute onion and green pepper in butter until tender. Add fish and rice, mix lightly. Blend soup and milk. Coat the bottom of a well-greased 2 quart casserole with 1/2 cup crumbs. Cover with alternate layers of fish and soup mixture. Top with remaining crumbs. Bake for 20—30 minutes.

Carp Lasagne

1 lb. cooked carp, flaked
1 Tbsp. olive oil
1 cup onion, chopped
1 clove garlic, minced
1 can (1 lb.) tomatoes, peeled
1 can (8 oz.) tomato sauce
1 tsp. salt
1/4 tsp. pepper

1/4 tsp. dried rosemary
3/4 lb. lasagne noodles,
  freshly cooked
1/2 lb. mozzarella cheese
  grated
1/2 lb. ricotta cheese
  grated
1/2 cup Parmesan cheese,
  grated

Preheat oven to 350 degrees. Heat olive oil in large, heavy skillet and lightly saute onion and garlic. Add canned tomatoes, tomato sauce and seasonings, stir well. Cover and simmer for 20 minutes or until ingredients are blended and sauce is thick. Add fish, blend carefully and pour 1/4 of mixture over bottom of baking dish (8" by 12"). Arrange 1/3 lasagna noodles over sauce, spread 1/3 mozzarella and ricotta cheese over lasagna noodles. Repeat layers 2 more times and top with remaining fish-tomato sauce. Sprinkle with grated Parmesan and bake uncovered for 30 minutes. Remove from oven and let stand 15 minutes before cutting.

Catfish and Noodles

4 lbs. catfish fillets
3 cups cooked noodles
1/2 cup butter
1 cup flour

1 Tbsp. salt
1 tsp. pepper
6 strips bacon
6 olives

Preheat oven to 350 degrees. Combine flour, salt, pepper, and fillets in to a small plastic bag, shake well. Remove fillets and fry in hot butter until golden. Remove and towel dry. Position one strip of bacon and one olive on each fillet with toothpick. Bake for 15 minutes. Serve with noodles.

Catfish in the Oven

2 lbs. catfish fillets
3/4 cup fresh parsley, chopped
3/4 cup onion, chopped
3/4 cup celery leaves, chopped
1 clove garlic, minced
1/4 tsp. thyme

1/2 tsp. salt
1/2 tsp. ground pepper
1 cup white wine
3 Tbsp. lemon juice
3 Tbsp. oil

Preheat oven to 325 degrees. Mix finely chopped parsley, green onions, celery leaves, garlic, and thyme. Put half of the mixture in a bowl, add salt and pepper. Pour in the wine, lemon juice and oil, mix. Spread the other half of mixture in bottom of baking dish. Place catfish fillets on top. Pour mixture in bowl over fish. Cover and bake for 30 minutes or until fish flakes easily.

Cheesey Baked Walleye

1 1/2 lbs. walleye fillets
1/4 cup butter, melted
1 clove garlic, minced
1 can sliced water chestnuts
1 can cream of celery soup
   (mixed with 1/4 cup milk)

1/4 tsp. salt
1/8 tsp. pepper
2 cups bread crumbs mixed with
   1/2 lb. finely shredded
   cheddar cheese

Preheat oven to 350 degrees. Place butter and garlic an a shallow baking dish. Place fillets in the dish and brush with butter. Cover the fillets with sliced water chestnuts and pour soup over the top. Add salt and pepper. Sprinkle with bread crumbs and bake about 25 minutes.

Chipped Perch

2 lbs. perch fillets
2 cups caesar salad dressing
1 cup crushed potato chips

1/2 cup Sharp Cheddar cheese
  shredded

Preheat oven to 500 degrees. Dip fillets in salad dressing. Place fillets in a single layer, skin side down, in a baking pan. Combine crushed chips and cheese, sprinkle over fillets. Bake for 10—15 minutes or until fillets flake easily with a fork.

Cod Steaks with Mushroom Sauce

4 fresh codfish steaks
   3/4" thick
1 small onion, chopped
1/4 lb. mushrooms, chopped
6 Tbsp. boiling water

3 Tbsp. butter
3 Tbsp. flour
2 cups milk
salt and pepper
paprika

Preheat oven to 350 degrees. Place steaks in greased baking dish. Cook onion and mushrooms in water for 3 minutes. Melt butter in a saucepan. Add flour and heat for 3 minutes. In a separate saucepan, heat milk. Pour half the milk into the butter and flour mixture and stir until smooth. Now, pour rest of milk into mixture and whisk vigorously until smooth, stirring constantly until brought to a boil. Season and pour over cod. Sprinkle with paprika. Bake for about 30 to 35 minutes, until fish is tender.

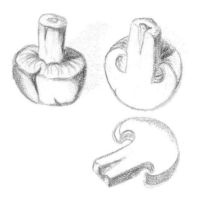

Coho Parmesan

2 lbs. coho fillets   1/4 tsp. salt
1/2 cup thick french dressing   1 can french fried onions
2 Tbsp. lemon juice   1/4 cup grated Parmesan cheese

Preheat oven to 350 degrees. Wash fish and cut into serving size pieces; place in a shallow baking dish. Combine dressing, lemon juice and salt. Pour sauce over fish and let stand for 30 minutes, turning at least once. Remove fish from sauce and place in a well greased shallow baking dish. Crush french fried onions and add cheese; mix thoroughly and sprinkle over fish. Bake for 25—30 minutes or until fish flakes easily with a fork.

Crappie Fillet Loaf

8 crappie fillets   salt and pepper
6 Tbsp. butter   1 1/2 cups sour cream
1 cup fine bread crumbs   2 Tbsp. fresh dill, chopped
6 white onions, thinly sliced   or dry dill weed

Preheat oven to 350 degrees. Butter sides and bottom of a loaf pan and line with bread crumbs. Alternate layers of fish and onion slices in pan, seasoning each layer with salt and pepper and covering each layer with sour cream, sprinkled with dill. The last layer should have a heavy covering of sour cream. Bake uncovered for 30 minutes or until golden brown. Loosen fish by running a table knife around the edge of pan allowing it to be removed as a loaf. Sprinkle with dill and cut in thick slices.

Crappie Fillets with Orange Butter

4 lbs. fresh crappie fillets   4 tsp. orange juice
4 tsp. grated orange rind   2 tsp. salt
6 Tbsp. melted butter   pepper to taste

Preheat oven to 450 degrees. Wash fillets and pat dry with paper towels. Spread fillets evenly in a greased pan. Mix other ingredients and pour over fish. Bake for 15 minutes or until fish flakes easily with a fork.

Crappie Souffle

1 lb. cooked fillets, flaked	1/4 tsp. salt
1 cup milk or white wine	1/4 tsp. nutmeg
3 Tbsp. butter	5 egg yolks
1 slice white bread, cubed	5 egg whites
1 tsp. prepared mustard	1/2 cup Parmesan cheese
paprika	

Preheat oven to 375 degrees. Heat the milk and butter until the butter is melted. Pour into a blender, add bread, mustard, salt, and nutmeg. Cover and blend for 5 seconds, then add flaked cooked fish and blend for 10 seconds. Add egg yolks and blend 15 seconds more. Beat the egg whites until stiff (but not dry) and carefully fold into fish mixture. Butter a souffle dish and fill to within 1/2 inch of the top, sprinkle with Parmesan cheese and a little paprika, set on cooking sheet and bake for 15-20 minutes until puffed and brown. Serve immediately.

Creamy Baked Northern

4 lbs. northern	1 onion, chopped
salt and pepper	2 cups sour cream
4 Tbsp. butter	1 cup tomato soup

Preheat oven to 425 degrees. Salt and pepper fish inside and out. Saute onion in melted butter. Place sauteed onion in cavity. Mix sour cream and soup in same skillet in which onion was sauted. Heat and pour over fish. Bake for about 45 minutes. Baste frequently. When serving, pour sauce over fish.

Crispy Baked Bass

2 lbs. bass fillets	1/2 cup evaporated milk
4 Tbsp. olive oil	1/2 cup water
1/2 tsp. salt	1 cup cornflakes, crushed
1/4 tsp. pepper	

Preheat oven to 350 degrees. Coat baking sheet heavily with olive oil. Add salt and pepper to evaporated milk and dilute with water. Put crushed cornflakes in shallow bowl, dip fillets in liquid, then coat with cornflakes. Place fillets on oiled sheet and bake for 15 minutes.

Crusty Oven-Baked Fish

2 lbs. fish fillets
1/2 cup wheat germ
1/2 cup peanut flour (raw
  peanuts ground in blender or
  nut grinder)
1/4 cup sesame seeds
1/2 cup bran flakes or whole
  grain bread crumbs

1 tsp. salt
1/2 tsp. black pepper
1/2 tsp. oregano
1/2 tsp. marjoram
1/2 tsp. paprika
1/2 tsp. garlic powder
1/2 cup oil
1/2 cup lemon juice
1 egg

Preheat oven to 400 degrees. Wash fish and pat dry with paper towels. Cut fish into serving size pieces. Combine all of the dry ingredients to make a crumb mixture and set aside. Combine egg, oil and lemon juice and beat well. Dip portions of fish into egg mixture and then into crumbs. Place in shallow baking pan which has been lightly oiled. Bake for about 20 minutes, or until tender.

Delicious Baked Fish

1 lb. cod fillets (trout
  or sole can also be used)
salt and pepper
1/4 cup salad oil
3 Tbsp. water

1 tsp. lemon juice
1/2 cup fine bread crumbs
2 tsp. parsley, chopped
1 Tbsp. oregano

Preheat oven to 400 degrees. Place fish in well greased pan and sprinkle with salt and pepper. Mix together the salad oil, water and lemon juice. Pour over the fish. Add the bread crumbs, parsley and oregano. Bake for about 30 minutes, or until fish flakes easily with a fork.

Delicious Baked Trout

4 dressed trout
1 tsp. Worcestershire sauce
1 tsp. prepared mustard
3 Tbsp. lemon juice

1 1/2 cups sour cream
1 cup onion, chopped
salt and pepper

Preheat oven to 350 degrees. Line a baking pan with foil. Rub trout with salt and pepper. Mix Worcestershire sauce, mustard, lemon juice, sour cream, onion, salt and pepper. Fill fish with some sauce and pour remaining sauce over fish. Bake for 60 minutes, basting occasionally.

Deviled Panfish

4 lbs. panfish (drop fillets
   in boiling water, remove
   and drain)
1 cup milk
1/2 cup butter
1 1/2 Tbsp. onion, grated
dash pepper
3 Tbsp. Worcestershire sauce
crumbled corn flakes

1 green pepper, diced
4 thick slices white bread
   (crust removed)
3 Tbsp. parsley, chopped
3/4 tsp. salt
dash hot sauce
1 tsp. dry mustard
1 pimiento, finely chopped

Preheat oven to 350 degrees. Cook everything but the fish and cornflakes for 10 minutes, stirring constantly. Add the fish and cook another 5 minutes. Place in a casserole, sprinkle lightly with crumbled corn flakes. Brown in oven for 10—15 minutes.

Easy Baked Bass

6 fillets (6—8 oz. ea.)   1/4 cup melted butter
1/4 tsp. seasoning, your choice   1 onion, thinly sliced
1/2 tsp. salt

Preheat oven to 350 degrees. Place bass fillets in single layer in shallow baking pan. Mix seasoning into butter and pour over fish. Bake for about 12 minutes. Remove from oven and layer with sliced onions. Spoon drippings over top and return to oven for 5—10 minutes, until fish flakes easily.

Fillet Au Gratin

1 lb. fresh fish fillets   4 cups water
5 Tbsp. oil   nutmeg, salt, and kelp powder
4 Tbsp. brown rice flour   to taste
2 Tbsp. soy flour   4 egg yolks
4 tsp. cornstarch   4 egg whites
1 cup skim milk powder   4 Tbsp. wheat germ

Preheat oven to 300 degrees. Brush fillets with 1 tablespoon of the oil and bake for 15-20 minutes, until tender. Increase oven temperature to 350 degrees. Sift together rice and soy flours. Put 4 tablespoons oil into a saucepan and stir in flours. Heat until it bubbles. Combine skim milk powder and water using a wire whisk. Add slowly to oil-flour mixture, stirring constantly. Cook until sauce is thickened and flours no longer have their raw taste. Season with nutmeg, salt, and kelp powder. Beat egg yolks and slowly add a little of the hot sauce to them, stirring. Stir egg yolk-mixture into hot sauce, and continue to stir for one minute more. Remove from heat. Break cooked flounder into bite-size pieces and add to sauce. Beat egg whites until stiff. Fold them into fish mixture. Pour into casserole, top with wheat germ and bake for 30 minutes or until the au gratin has set.

Fillets Florentine

1 1/2—2 lbs. panfish fillets	1/2 tsp. salt
1 small package frozen spinach	6 slices bacon
chopped or leaf	1/2 tsp. lemon-pepper seasoning
1/4 tsp. ground nutmeg	2/3 cup sour cream

Preheat oven to 350 degrees. Thaw spinach and drain well. Grease a baking dish and place the drained spinach in the bottom of the dish. Sprinkle with nutmeg and salt. Cook the bacon until it is crisp, then crumble and sprinkle half on top of spinach. Place the fillets on top of the spinach, sprinkle with lemon-pepper seasoning, drizzle with some of the bacon grease and spread with sour cream, covering fillets well. Sprinkle the top with crumbled bacon and bake for 15—20 minutes or until fish flakes easily.

Fish and Dressing

4 fish steaks, 1" thick	1/2 tsp. salt
(about 2 lbs.)	1/4 tsp. pepper
1 stalk celery, chopped	1/4 tsp. ground sage
1 onion, chopped	1 egg, slightly beaten
1/4 cup butter	1/2 tsp. salt
1 can (4 oz.) mushroom stems	2 Tbsp. lemon juice
and pieces	paprika
1 medium carrot, shredded	1/4 cup snipped parsley

2 cups unseasoned croutons, coursely crushed Preheat oven 350 degrees. In a 2 quart sauce pan, melt butter, then cook and stir onion and celery over medium heat until celery is tender; remove from heat. Stir in mushrooms (with liquid), croutons, carrot, parsley, salt, pepper, sage and egg.

Place fish steaks in greased jelly roll pan (15 1/2 x 10 1/2 x 1); sprinkle with 1/2 teaspoons salt, lemon juice, and paprika. Spoon crouton mixture around fish. Bake, uncovered, 35 to 40 minutes until fish flakes easily with a fork.

Fish and Sweet Potatoes

1 lb. fish fillets
1 can (16 or 17 oz.) sweet
  potatoes
1/2 cup apricot preserves

2 Tbsp. catsup
2 Tbsp. lemon juice
2 green onion, with tops,
  chopped

Oven-fry the fish at 425 degrees in casserole dish. Remove from oven. Arrange sweet potatoes around fish. Mix preserves, catsup and lemon juice; brush on fish and potatoes. Bake uncovered until potatoes are hot, about 15 minutes. Sprinkle with green onions.

Fish Balls

1 lb. ground northern
1 cup bread crumbs

salt and pepper

Salt and pepper fish then add bread crumbs, mixing well. Form fish mixture into balls about 1 inch in diameter. Set aside.

Prepared white sauce: (for 1 lb. fish balls)

4 Tbsp. butter
4 Tbsp. flour

2 cups milk
salt and pepper

Preheat oven to 300 degrees. Melt butter over low heat in saucepan or double boiler. Add flour and continue to cook for 3 minutes, stirring constantly. Remove from heat and slowly stir in the milk. Return the pan to heat and bring to a boil, stirring continuously. Place mixture in a double boiler, add salt and pepper, and cook until mixture thickens. Beat with a hand mixer or egg beater, until smooth. Place the fish balls in a baking dish or casserole and completely cover with the white sauce. Place in oven and bake for 1 1/2 hours.

Fish Cheese Bake

2 1/2 lbs. pike or bass
1 onion, chopped
1/2 lb. American cheese,
 grated
1 1/2 tsp. Worcestershire sauce

1 tsp. mustard
1 tsp. salt
1/4 tsp. pepper
1 cup milk

Preheat oven to 425 degrees. Spread half the cheese and the onion over the bottom of a baking dish. Place fish on top and cover with remaining cheese. Combine remaining ingredients and pour over cheese. Bake for 25 to 30 minutes.

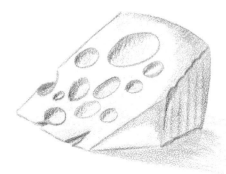

Fish Divine

1 lb. fish fillets
2 packages (10 oz. ea.)
 frozen broccoli spears
1 tsp. salt

1 can (10 3/4 oz.) condensed
 cream of chicken soup
1/2 cup milk
1 can (3 oz.) french fried
 onions

Preheat oven to 350 degrees. Let fish
tand at room temperature for 10 minutes then cut into 5 equal parts. R
nse broccoli under cold running water to separate; drain. (If brocco
i stems are more than 1/2 inch in diameter, cut lengthwise into halves.)
Place fish in center of ungreased 13 x 9 x 2 inch baking dish. Arrange broccoli around fish. Sprinkle with salt. Mix soup and milk pour over fish and broccoli. Bake uncovered for about 30 minutes, until fish flakes easily with a fork. Sprinkle with onions and bake 5 minutes longer.

Fish Fillets with Crab Meat

2 lbs. fillets
3 green onions, chopped
3 oz. mushrooms, chopped
1 Tbsp. butter
2 cups chicken stock
salt and pepper

1 cup crab meat
4 Tbsp. butter
1/2 tsp. salt
1 egg yolk
1 lemon, sliced
1/3 cup white wine

Preheat oven to 425 degrees. To make sauce: cook onions and mushrooms in 1 tablespoon butter. Cook until tender. Mix in flour, add stock, season and cook 5 minutes. Add half of the wine.

Saute fillets and crab meat separately in butter for 5 minutes. Add the remaining wine, salt and slightly beaten egg yolk to crab meat and cook until thickened, stirring constantly. Place some of the crab meat mixture on half of each fillet. Fold the other half of fillet over crab meat mixture; cover with sauce. Place in cooking bag and bake about 10 minutes. Arrange on platter and garnish with lemon slices.

Fish Florentine

6 fish fillets (about 1 1/2 lbs.)
1/4 cup onion, chopped
1/8 tsp. dill, crushed
2 Tbsp. oil
1/2 cup cooked brown rice

1/4 cup toasted almonds
    chopped
1 tsp. lemon juice
1 1/2 lbs. fresh spinach,
    chopped

Preheat oven to 350 degrees. Saute onions and dill in oil until tender. Add spinach and saute until wilted, (about 3 minutes). Add rice, almonds and lemon juice; cook and stir occasionally. Place 1/4 cup of the mixture on each fillet. Roll and close ends securely. Place in greased, shallow baking dish. Bake for 20 minutes.

Fish Loaf

2 1/2 cups (boned) raw
   fish, diced
1 tsp. dried onion
1 Tbsp. lemon juice
1 tsp. salt
1/2 tsp. pepper
1 can cream of mushroom soup

2 cups dry bread (soak in water
   and squeeze out)
1 can mushrooms
1 Tbsp. paprika
2 eggs, beaten
1/2 cup celery, diced

Preheat oven to 375 degrees. Mix all ingredients together, form into loaf
shape, place in greased loaf pan and bake for 45 minutes.

Fish Roll

1 1/2 cups cooked fish, flaked
baking powder biscuit dough
   (using 2 cups flour)
1 small onion, chopped

1 green pepper, chopped
1/2 tsp. salt
milk

Preheat oven to 400 degrees. Roll biscuit dough to 1/4 inch thickness on floured board. Combine fish, onion, green pepper and salt; moisten slightly with milk. Mix well and spread mixture on dough. Roll as for jelly roll and cut into 1 1/2 inch slices. Bake on greased cooking sheet for 30 minutes.

Fish Souffle

2 cups cooked, flaked fish
1/4 cup butter
1/4 cup flour
1 tsp. salt
1/4 tsp. pepper

1/2 tsp. chili powder
5 eggs
2 Tbsp. sherry wine
dry bread crumbs
horseradish

Preheat oven to 375 degrees. Melt butter in a saucepan and blend flour into it. Slowly add milk, stirring constantly until it is smooth and thickened. Separate eggs. Beat yolks. Slowly beat the milk mixture into the yolks. Add fish, sherry, salt, pepper, chili powder and mix. Beat egg whites until stiff and glossly. With a wooden spoon, fold egg whites into the fish mixture. Pour into a greased 1 1/2 quart casserole. Sprinkle with bread crumbs. Bake in oven for 45 minutes or until a knife inserted in the center comes out clean. Serve with horseradish.

Fish Steaks Creole

1 1/2 lbs. fish steaks
1 green pepper, chopped
1 small onion, chopped
1/2 cup celery, chopped
2 Tbsp. butter

1 tsp. salt
1/2 tsp. pepper
1/2 cup bread crumbs
2 tsp. butter, melted
1 cup tomatoes, chopped

Preheat oven to 375 degrees. Place fish in well-greased baking pan. Saute green pepper, onion and celery in 2 tablespoons butter or margarine. Add tomatoes and cook for 5 minutes; sprinkle with salt and pepper. Place this over the fish, then sprinkle with bread crumbs which have been moistened with the melted butter. Bake for 30 minutes.

Fish—Wine Casserole

2 lbs. of fish fillets or
  steaks (salmon, swordfish,
  flounder) thawed if frozen
4 Tbsp. butter, plus 1 tsp. for
  baking dish
1/2 lb. mushrooms, fresh,
  chopped, or 4—6 oz.
  can, drained
2 Tbsp. parsley, minced

1/2 tsp. salt
1/4 tsp. pepper
1/2 cup dry wine, red or white
1 cup clam juice
1 small onion, minced
1/4 cup milk
4 Tbsp. grated cheese
1 tsp. paprika
4 Tbsp. flour

Preheat oven to 375 degrees. Wash fish and dry on towels. Place a layer of fillets or steaks in a large, buttered baking dish.

Melt 4 tablespoons of butter in a large pan. Add the mushrooms, stirring occasionally over medium heat, until they are soft; add flour and mix. Sprinkle with parsley, salt and pepper, stir with a wire whisk add wine and clam juice. Bring to a boil, add the onion and milk. Simmer with cover on for about 5 minutes, stirring once or twice.

Pour sauce over fish in the baking dish. Sprinkle with cheese and paprika. Bake uncovered, until fish is tender and flakes easily. About 15 minutes for fillets, 30 minutes for steaks.

Fish with Chili Sauce

2 lbs. fish fillets 1/4 cup grated Parmesan cheese 1 tsp. salt 1 lb. zucchini, cut crosswise Tomato-Chili Sauce (See Below) into 1/4" slices 1/2 tsp. garlic salt

Preheat oven to 475 degrees. Arrange fish in ungreased (11 x 7 x 1 x 1 1/2") baking dish. Sprinkle with salt. Spread 1 tablespoon Tomato-Chili Sauce over each piece of fish. Sprinkle with 2 tablespoons of cheese. Arrange zucchini slice on fish; sprinkle with garlic salt and remaining cheese. Bake uncovered for about 1 hour or until fish flakes easily with fork. Serve with remaining Tomato-Chili sauce.

Chili Sauce:

1 bottle (12 oz.) chili sauce	1 Tbsp. lemon juice
	1/2 tsp. Worcestershire sauce
1 Tbsp. prepared horseradish	1/4 tsp. salt

Mix all ingredients and bring to a boil, stirring occasionally.

Fish with Sour Cream

1 lb. fish fillets	1/2 cup sour cream
4 oz. mushrooms, sliced	3 Tbsp. grated Parmesan cheese
1 small onion, chopped	2 Tbsp. dry bread crumbs
1 Tbsp. butter or margarine	paprika
1/2 tsp. salt	snipped parsley
1/8 tsp. pepper	

Preheat oven to 350 degrees. Wash fish. If fillets are large, cut into serving pieces. Pat fish dry with paper towels; arrange in ungreased (12 x 7 1/2 x 2") baking dish. Cook mushrooms and onions in butter until mushrooms are tender, about 3 minutes. Spoon mushroom mixture over fish; sprinkle with salt and pepper.

Blend sour cream and cheese; spread over mushroom mixture. Sprinkle with bread crumbs. Bake uncovered for 25 to 30 minutes, until fish flakes easily with fork. Sprinkle with paprika and parsley.

Foil Baked Perch

2 lbs. perch fillets
1 can condensed milk

1 cup bread crumbs
finely ground

Preheat oven to 350 degrees. Dip fillets in condensed milk, then into bread crumbs. Lay on oiled aluminum foil and place in oven for 25 to 30 minutes. Garnish with lemon and parsley.

Gingersnap Carp

2 lbs. carp, sliced
1/3 cup cooking oil
2 onions, sliced
2 carrots, sliced

5 gingersnaps
1 1/2 cups warm water
1/2 tsp. whole mixed spices
1/4 tsp. salt

Preheat oven to 325 degrees. Pour half of oil in baking dish, arrange half of fish on top, cover with half of onions and carrots. Add remaining fish and vegetables. Put gingersnaps in water and stir until smooth. Add spices and salt and pour over fish. Add remaining oil and more water to cover fish. Cover dish and bake about 1 hour.

Grandma's Walleye Dish

8 walleye fillets (2 lbs.)
2 Tbsp. lemon juice
salt and pepper
1/4 cup green onions, finely
    chopped
1/4 cup mushrooms, chopped

2 Tbsp. parsley, finely chopped
3 Tbsp. butter
4—5 medium tomatoes (or a
    1 lb. can)
1 cup dry white wine

Preheat oven to 350 degrees. Sprinkle lemon juice on fillets, season lightly with salt and pepper. Saute onions, mushrooms and parsley in butter. Peel and dice tomatoes, removing seeds; toss in a bowl and add sauteed onions, mushrooms and parsley. Place fillets in stovetop, oven-proof baking dish. Pour tomato, onion, mushroom, parsley mixture over the top. Add 1 cup white wine. Bake until fish flakes easily with fork.

Herb-Butter Fish

1 1/2—2 lbs. fish fillets
1/2 cup soft butter
1/4 cup parsley, minced
1 tsp. onion, grated

1/2 tsp. thyme
1/2 tsp. dry mustard
few drops of hot sauce
1/2 tsp. Worcestershire sauce

Preheat oven to 350 degrees. Place fillets in a greased baking dish. Combine butter with remaining ingredients; spread on fish. Bake for 25 to 30 minutes. Baste twice during baking.

Herring Roll-Ups

6 salt herring
2 Tbsp. bread crumbs
2 Tbsp. butter
1 Tbsp. parsley, chopped

1 1/2 Tbsp. lemon juice
pepper
hot water

Preheat oven to 375 degrees. Soak herring in cold water overnight, in refrigerator. Drain and clean by removing skin. Separate each fish into 2 fillets, removing bones. Mix remaining ingredients to a smooth paste. Spread each fillet with paste, roll, fasten with a string or toothpicks and place in a baking dish. Cover with oiled wax paper and bake for 10 to 15 minutes. Remove string or toothpicks. Serve.

Italian Baked Fish

4—6 lbs. fresh fish fillets
2 onions, thinly sliced
3 cups tomatoes (fresh or canned)
   drained and coarsely chopped
1/2 tsp. coriander, ground
1/2 tsp. fennel, ground

1/2 tsp. basil
1/2 tsp. oregano
1 clove garlic, minced
1/2 tsp. salt
pepper to taste

Preheat oven to 350 degrees. Layer fillets with onions in a baking pan. Combine remaining ingredients. Pour over fish. Bake uncovered, for 50 minutes to 1 hour until fish is tender and onions are done.

Lake Trout with Cheese

4 lbs. lake trout fillets
1 tsp. salt
1/4 tsp. pepper
6 cups soft bread cubes
1/2 cup parsley, chopped

3/4 cup melted bacon fat
2 cups onions, chopped
2 tsp. dried mustard
2 cups cheddar cheese, grated

Preheat oven to 350 degrees. Place fillets in greased baking dish and season with salt and pepper. Melt butter and add onions, saute until tender. Toast bread cubes. Stir together; bread cubes, butter and onion mixture, and mustard. Add cheese and parsley; toss until well mixed. Spread over fillets and bake for 20 minutes.

Lake Trout with Rice Stuffing

1 lake trout (4—10 lbs.)
salt
3/4 cup onion, chopped
1 cup celery, diced
1/4 cup butter
1 1/3 cups rice, cooked

1 cup stuffed olives, chopped
1/4 tsp. salt
1/4 tsp. pepper
1/4 tsp. sage
1/2 tsp. thyme
melted butter for basting

Preheat oven to 450 degrees. Wash fish thoroughly and pat dry with paper towels. Salt cavity. Saute onions and celery in butter. Add rice, olives, salt, pepper, sage and thyme and mix thoroughly. Allow about 3/4 cup of stuffing per pound of dressed fish. Stuff loosely. Close with skewers or by sewing. Place stuffed fish in a greased roasting pan. Brush well with melted butter. Measure stuffed fish at the thickest depth and allow 10 minutes per inch cooking time.

Largemouth Almondine

2 lbs. fresh bass fillets
1/2 cup butter

1/2 cup white wine
3/4 cup almond slivers

Preheat oven to 350 degrees. Melt butter in shallow baking dish Season fish with salt and pepper to taste. Dip both sides of fillets in butter and place in baking dish. In a small saucepan bring wine to a boil and pour over fillets. Bake about 25 minutes or until fish flakes easily. Sprinkle with slivered almonds and serve.

New Orleans Baked Salmon

2 lbs. whole salmon
1 tsp. sugar
1/8 tsp. salt
dash pepper
1 clove garlic
1 red pepper pod
1 onion, minced

2 1/2 cups cooked tomatoes
1 Tbsp. Worcestershire sauce
1/2 cup olive oil
1 Tbsp. vinegar
2 cups uncooked tater tots
1 cup mushrooms

Preheat oven to 400 degrees. Brown sugar in pan. Sprinkle salmon with salt and pepper. Place garlic and pepper pod inside cavity. Place salmon and onion in pan with sugar. Cover with tomatoes; add Worcestershire sauce, olive oil, vinegar and potatoes. Bake for 15 minutes; add mushrooms and bake another 15 minutes or longer until fish and potatoes are tender.

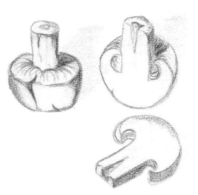

Northern Steaks in Horseradish Sauce

1 1/2 lbs. northern pike cut
  into steaks
1 cup sour cream
3 Tbsp. milk
1 Tbsp. cream style white
  horseradish

2 Tbsp. lemon juice
1 tsp. capers with juice
1 tsp. dry mustard
2 Tbsp. fresh parsley, chopped
salt and pepper
3 Tbsp. butter

Preheat oven to 350 degrees. Sprinkle the pike with salt and pepper. Melt the butter in a baking dish and coat both sides of fillets in it. Pour horseradish sauce over the fish (see below). Bake uncovered for 25 minutes, or until fish is tender. Garnish with lemon wedges or fresh parsley.

Horseradish Sauce: Combine sour cream, milk, horseradish, lemon juice, capers, dry mustard and parsley.

Oriental Fish with Sesame Seeds

1 lb. fish fillets, cut into
   1″ x 2″ serving pieces
1/2 cup sesame seeds
1/4 cup soy sauce

3—4 green onions, cut into
   small slices
2 Tbsp. oil

Preheat oven to 350 degrees. Heat sesame seeds in small fry pan, stirring frequently. Remove when golden, but not brown. Combine onions, soy sauce and oil. Dip fish pieces in the soy mixture, then roll in the toasted sesame seeds.

Place fish pieces on broiler pan, then place in center of oven. Cook approximately 6 to 10 minutes. Time varies according to thickness of fillets. Fish is done when the meat turns white and flakes easily.

Oriental Trout

4 trout (8 to 10 oz. each)
3 green onions
2 stalks celery, sliced
2 Tbsp. cooking oil
1/4 lb. mushrooms, sliced

1 cup green pepper, sliced
1 cup bean sprouts
4 eggs
2 tsp. soy sauce
8 strips bacon

Preheat oven to 500 degrees. Cut onions into 1 1/2 inch pieces. Slice celery at an angle, 1/4 inch thick. Heat oil in wok or cast iron skillet. Stir-fry mushrooms, green pepper, onions, bean sprouts and celery for two minutes. Add soy sauce to slightly beaten egg, then add to vegetable mixture. Continue to toss mixture until eggs start to cook slightly. Stuff each of the trout with 1/4 of the mixture; wrap with 2 slices bacon, tucking ends under fish. Bake in large pan for 12 to 15 minutes. Skin should be crisp and flesh opaque to the bone.

Oven-Fried Fish

2 lbs. fillets	2 tsp. salt
1 cup milk	1 cup finely crushed crackers
4 tsp. melted butter	

Preheat oven to 500 degrees. Cut fillets into serving size pieces. Add salt to milk. Dip fish in milk, then roll in crumbs. Place fish in well greased shallow baking pan; drizzle with melted butter. Place on top rack of very hot oven. Bake for 10 to 15 minutes, until fish is brown.

Oven Walleye in Wine Sauce

8 walleye fillets	1/2 Tbsp. lemon juice
2 Tbsp. butter, melted	salt and pepper
1 cup mushrooms, finely sliced	3/4 cup white wine
2 Tbsp. green onions, minced	3/4 cup chicken stock

Wine Sauce:

2 Tbsp. butter, melted	salt and pepper
2 1/2 Tbsp. flour	1 Tbsp. fresh parsley, minced
1/2 cup whipping cream	1 Tbsp. fresh chives, minced

Preheat oven to 350 degrees. Cook sliced mushrooms and green onion slowly in butter and lemon juice in covered pan until mushrooms are limp but not brown. Season lightly with salt and pepper. Place 4 walleye fillets in buttered baking dish; season with salt and pepper. Divide cooked mushrooms and green onions over the fillets, cover with remaining fillets. Pour wine and chicken stock with juices from mushroom pan around the fish. Liquid should almost cover fish, add more wine if needed. Put a piece of buttered wax paper on top of fish.

Bring to simmer on top of stove. Place in oven for 12 minutes. Remove from oven. Drain poaching liquid into sauce pan. Keep fish warm. Reduce liquid to 1 cup by boiling. Stir melted butter into flour in second saucepan. Cook slowly until it foams but remains yellow. Remove from heat, blend in reduced poaching liquid. Beat in whipping cream and bring to slow boil, stirring constantly. Thin with more cream, if necessary. Add salt and pepper or a few more drops of lemon juice, if needed. Spoon over fish, top with minced parsley and chives.

Paddlefish Casserole

2 cups cooked paddlefish,
   flaked
2 cups cooked rice
1 cup milk
3 Tbsp. melted butter

dash of black pepper
1 can cream of celery soup or
   cream of mushroom soup
1 cup fine bread crumbs

Preheat oven to 375 degrees. Layer rice in a 2 quart casserole, then add the flaked paddlefish. Sprinkle with a little pepper. Blend milk and soup, pour over fish and rice. Blend bread crumbs and melted butter and sprinkle over top of milk and soup mixture. Bake for 25 - 30 minutes or until crumbs are golden brown.

Parmesan Walleye

1 1/2 lb. walleye fillets
   cut into pieces
1/4 cup melted butter
1/2 tsp. salt
1/4 tsp. white pepper

1 Tbsp. lemon juice
4 Tbsp. Parmesan cheese
1/4 tsp. garlic powder
1/4 tsp. paprika

Preheat oven to 425 degrees. Place butter in a 9 x 13" baking pan. Lay fillets in the pan and sprinkle with salt and pepper. Bake for about 6 minutes then carefully turn fillets. Dribble with lemon juice, then sprinkle with Parmesan, garlic, paprika mixture. Return to the oven and bake until fish flakes easily with a fork.

Perch and Pineapple

1 lb. perch fillets
1/2 cup pineapple juice
1 Tbsp. lime juice

2 tsp. Worcestershire sauce
1/2 tsp. salt
dash pepper

Cut fish into serving-size portions. Place in a shallow baking dish.

Combine pineapple juice, lime juice, Worcestershire sauce, salt and a dash of pepper. Pour over fish. Marinate for 1 hour in refrigerator, turning once.

Bake until fish flakes easily with fork.

Perch with Orange Rice Stuffing

4 pan-dressed perch
2 Tbsp. butter
3/4 cup Budweiser beer
1/2 cup orange juice
1/2 tsp. salt
2 Tbsp. melted butter

1/2 cup chopped celery
1/2 cup uncooked brown rice
1/2 tsp. grated orange peel
1 tsp. lemon juice
1 Tbsp. chopped parsley
2 Tbsp. orange juice

Saute celery in butter in medium skillet until tender. Stir in rice, Budweiser beer, orange peel, 1/2 cup orange juice, lemon juice and salt. Bring to a boil; cover and reduce heat. Simmer until rice is tender, 15 to 20 minutes; stir in parsley. Sprinkle fish cavities with salt; stuff each fish with about 1/2 cup rice mixture. Skewer closed; place fish in a greased, shallow baking pan. Combine melted butter and 2 tablespoons orange juice; brush over fish. Bake, uncovered, at 350 degrees about 30 minutes or until fish flakes easily with fork. Baste with melted butter and orange juice mixture while baking.

Quick Baked Fish Fillets

1 lb. fish fillets
2/3 cup condensed soup your:
   choice: tomato, mushroom,
   celery or asparagus

2 Tbsp. dry white wine
2 Tbsp. milk
cayenne pepper (small pinch)

Preheat oven to 350 degrees. Place fish in baking dish. Mix milk with soup, heat and stir until smooth. Add cayenne and pour over fish. Bake 30 minutes or until fish is tender. Suggestions: Serve with rice.

Rainbows with Mushrooms

6 dressed rainbow trout
2 tsp. salt
4 cups soft bread cubes
2/3 cup butter
1 cup mushrooms, sliced

2/3 cup green onions, sliced
1/4 cup parsley, chopped
2 Tbsp. pimiento, chopped
1/2 tsp. marjoram

Preheat oven to 350 degrees. Lightly salt inside of trout. Saute bread cubes in 1/2 cup butter until lightly browned; add mushrooms and green onions; saute until mushrooms are tender. Stir in salt, parsley, pimiento, lemon juice and marjoram. Toss lightly. Stuff fish and arrange in a single layer in greased baking pan. Brush with remaining melted butter and bake for 25 to 30 minutes, or until fish flakes easily with fork.

Rolled Fish Fillets

1 or 2 fillets per person   1/3 cup mayonnaise
1 envelope dry sour cream mix   1 tsp. onion, minced

Preheat oven to 350 degrees. Prepare sour cream mix as directed on package. Mix with mayonnaise and onions. Roll fillets and place in greased baking dish or casserole. Pour sour cream mixture over fish. Cover and bake for 30 minutes.

Salmon Corn Pie

1 lb. salmon, boiled   2 cups milk
3 Tbsp. butter   2 Tbsp. onion, minced
1/2 tsp. salt   1 cup grated cheese
1/4 tsp. pepper   1 can corn, drained
1/2 cup buttered crumbs

Preheat oven to 375 degrees. Make a white sauce with the butter, flour, seasonings and milk. Flake the salmon and pick out any bones. Place 1/3 of salmon in buttered casserole, then add 1/3 of the sauce and sprinkle with 1/3 of the cheese. Repeat the layers twice. Spoon corn over cheese and top with the buttered crumbs. Bake for about 20 minutes.

Salmon and Vegetables

1 lb. salmon   2 cups cooked potatoes, diced
2 Tbsp. onions, diced   salt and pepper
2 Tbsp. butter   1/2 cup sour cream
2 cups cooked peas

Preheat oven to 350 degrees. Cook onion in butter until tender but not browned. Add liquid from salmon and peas and cook until liquid is reduced to about 1/2 cup. Place potatoes in shallow baking dish, add peas and sprinkle with salt and pepper. Break salmon into pieces and arrange on top of vegetables. Add liquid from vegetables to sour cream and mix until smooth. Pour over vegetables and fish. Bake for 40 minutes or until most of the liquid has been absorbed by vegetables.

Salmon Custard

1 lb. salmon, flaked
2 eggs, slightly beaten
1 cup evaporated milk

dash pepper
paprika
1/2 tsp. salt

Preheat oven to 350 degrees. Combine eggs, milk and seasonings; add salmon. Pour into baking dish, set in a pan of hot water for 25 to 30 minutes, until firm.

Salmon Fondue

1 cup cooked, flaked salmon
5 slices bread
1 cup milk
2 Tbsp. butter

3 eggs, separated
1/2 tsp. salt
1/4 cup American cheese,
   grated

Preheat oven to 350 degrees. Trim crusts from bread and cut into 1/2 inch cubes. Heat milk in double boiler. Add bread cubes, butter, cooking liquid from salmon and well beaten egg yolks; season with salt and cook until thickened, stirring constantly. Remove from heat and stir in cheese. Cool for 15 minutes. Add salmon. Beat egg whites until stiff and fold into mixture. Pour into greased baking dish. Place dish in shallow pan of hot water and bake for 1 hour, or until knife inserted in center comes out clean.

Salmon in Potato Boats

1 lb. salmon, flaked
2 Tbsp. onion, minced
2 Tbsp. green pepper, minced
3 Tbsp. fat
1 cup condensed tomato soup
1/2 tsp. salt

1 tsp. lemon juice
3 cups mashed potatoes
1/2 cup bread crumbs
3 Tbsp. butter, melted
1 tsp. prepared mustard

Preheat oven to 400 degrees. Brown onion and green pepper in fat. Add soup and seasonings. Simmer for a few minutes; add salmon. Shape potatoes into 6 boats on buttered baking sheet and fill with salmon mixture. Tip with crumbs mixed with melted butter. Bake until crumbs are browned, about 15 minutes.

Salmon Loaf

12 oz. salmon
1/4 cup milk
3/4 cup soft bread crumbs
2 Tbsp. melted butter
1 egg

juice of 1 lemon
1 Tbsp. onion, finely minced
1/2 cup green pepper, finely
minced
salt and pepper

Preheat oven to 350 degrees. Flake the salmon, remove any bones. Scald the milk and add bread crumbs and butter. Let stand about 5 minutes, then beat until smooth and combine with salmon, egg yolk, seasonings and flavorings. Finally stir in beaten egg white. Put in greased loaf pan and bake for about 35 minutes. Unmold and serve hot with tomato sauce.

Salmon Rice Loaf

4 cups cooked salmon, flaked
1 cup cooked rice
3/4 cup toasted, buttered
bread crumbs
2 eggs, beaten
1/2 tsp salt

1/2 tsp. celery salt
1/8 tsp. pepper
1 Tbsp. onion, chopped
1 Tbsp. parsley, chopped
1 Tbsp. pimiento, chopped
2 tomatoes, cut in wedges

Preheat oven to 350 degrees. Combine ingredients, except for tomatoes, in order given and place in buttered ring mold. Bake for 30-40 minutes. Remove from oven and brush with melted butter. Turn onto serving platter and fill center with buttered peas and carrots. Garnish with tomato wedges. Serve with lemon-butter sauce.

Salmon Stuffed Potatoes

1 1/2 cups cooked, flaked salmon
6 medium potatoes
1/3 cup hot milk
1 egg, well beaten
1 tsp. salt

1/4 tsp. paprika
1 Tbsp. lemon juice
1/3 cup onions, minced
2 Tbsp. butter
buttered crumbs

Preheat oven to 350 degrees. Bake potatoes, remove from oven and split lengthwise into halves. Scoop out potatoes and mash. Add milk, egg, salt, paprika and lemon juice. Beat until light and fluffy. Fold in salmon and onions which have been sauteed in butter. Put this mixture into potato shells, sprinkle with buttered bread crumbs and bake for 20 minutes.

Salmon with Tarragon Dressing 67 (Make 1 day ahead)

1 whole salmon (6—8 lbs.)	1 Tbsp. tarragon, crushed
1 tsp. salt	2 Tbsp. lemon juice
dash pepper	1 Tbsp. onion, minced
3 Tbsp. butter	3/4 tsp. salt
1/2 small head lettuce	1/4 tsp. pepper
cherry tomatoes, lemon	2 cups mayonnaise
slices and parsley for garnish	

Preheat oven to 400 degrees. Sprinkle cavity with salt and pepper, then dot with butter. Cut fish in half crosswise.

Line a shallow baking pan (11 " by 15 ") with lettuce leaves and place both halves of fish on lettuce. Bake for 1 hour or until fish flakes easily. cool for 1/2 hour, then place in refrigerator and chill overnight.

To make the mask, mix the mayonnaise (or mayonnaise and sour cream), tarragon, lemon juice, onion, salt and pepper; blend well. Chill.

To serve fish, put the two halves together on a large serving platter. (You may need to cut a thin slice from each. Cut end to allow the two halves to fit together neatly). Spread half of the mayonnaise mixture over the surface of the fish. Spoon the remaining mayonnaise mixture into a bowl to serve with the fish.

For the first servings, cut down only to the backbone of the salmon; when the tip half has been completely served, carefully remove the spine and adjoining bones. The bottom side of the fish is then ready for second servings with the extra dressing. Garnish the whole fish with cherry tomatoes, lemon slices and parsley.

Scalloped Fish and Nuts

1 cup flaked, cooked fish	2 hard cooked eggs, minced
2 cups medium white sauce	cracker crumbs
1 cup finely chopped nuts	butter

Preheat oven to 350 degrees. Combine fish with white sauce, nuts and eggs. Pour into greased casserole, cover with cracker crumbs and dot with butter. Bake for 25 minutes, until crumbs are browned.

Six-Way Fish Cakes

1 1/2 lbs. frozen fish
3/4 cup hashbrowns, frozen
1 egg
pepper to taste

1 or 2 Tbsp. onion, grated
1 Tbsp. soy sauce
1 tsp. oil

Grind, chop or grate frozen fish. Add potatoes. Beat egg. Add onion, pepper, soy sauce and oil to egg. Add fish and potatoes, mix thoroughly. While cold, using 2—3 tablespoons of mixture make fish balls. For baking, place balls on lightly greased non-stick cookie sheet, flatten no more than 1/8 inch thick. Bake 5 minutes at 450 degrees. Remove, turn cakes and bake 5 minutes more. Cover bottom of pan with oil. Put fish balls in pan one at a time, flattening each time. Turn as soon as bottom is set. Fry 6 minutes, turning occasionally. Serve immediately, plain or with seafood sauce. May be reheated by placing on cookie sheet and heating 5 minutes in 450 degree oven.

Spinach-Stuffed Fish Rolls

8 small fish fillets (about 2 lbs.)
1 package (12 oz.) frozen
  spinach souffle
1 Tbsp. lemon juice

1/4 cup butter melted
2 packages (1 oz. ea.)
  hollandaise sauce mix

Preheat oven to 350 degrees. Thaw spinach souffle at room temperature for about 20 minutes. Cut souffle lengthwise into halves. Cut each piece crosswise into 4 pieces. Drizzle fish fillets with lemon juice. Place 1 piece of spinach souffle on fillet and roll up. Place fish rolls seam side down, in lightly-greased baking dish (13 by 9 by 2 ").

Drain any liquid from baking dish. Pour butter over fish rolls. Bake uncovered until fish flakes easily with a fork, about 30 to 35 minutes. Remove rolls with slotted spatula. Prepare sauce mix as directed on package. Spoon half of the sauce over fish rolls. Serve remaining sauce with fish rolls.

Striped Bass, Stuffed and Baked

1 whole striped (5—7 lbs.)
2 Tbsp. margarine
1 onion, chopped
1 tsp. parsley
1/2 tsp. paprika
1 cup mushrooms, chopped

1/4 cup chicken broth or
  bouillon
1/2 cup canned shrimp, chopped
1 1/2 cups bread crumbs
melted butter
1/2 cup dry white wine

Preheat oven to 350 degrees. Fry onion in butter over medium heat for 7 minutes. Add parsley, paprika, mushrooms, and chicken broth; simmer for about 5 minutes. Add shrimp, stir and remove from heat. Add bread crumbs and enough wine to moisten the stuffing. Fill fish cavity with stuffing and secure with thread or skewers. Place fish in a large roasting pan and brush with melted butter. Add 1/2 cup of wine to pan. Bake fish for about 55 minutes until it flakes with a fork. If necessary, add more wine during cooking to keep the fish moist.

Striper and Broccoli

1 1/2 lbs. striper fillets
3 cups fresh broccoli, cut
  into bite-sized pieces
2 Tbsp. butter
salt and pepper

1 can cheddar cheese soup
1/3 cup light cream
dash of hot sauce
paprika
parsley sprigs

Preheat oven to 375 degrees. Butter baking dish and place broccoli on bottom. Sprinkle with salt and pepper and dot with butter. Add fillets. Heat soup, cream, and hot sauce to boiling point, then pour over the fillets and sprinkle with paprika. Cover with foil and place in oven for 35 minutes, until fish flakes easily with fork. Garnish with parsley.

Sweet-and-Sour Salmon

4 lbs. salmon fillets
seasoning salt
pepper

1 green pepper, cut in rings
1 medium onion, cut in rings

Preheat oven to 375 degrees. Place salmon fillets in 9" by 12" baking dish. Sprinkle with seasoning salt, and pepper. Cover pan with foil. Bake for 20 minutes. Remove from oven, add vegetables, cover and bake for another 20 minutes or more.

Sweet Basil Bass

2 lbs. bass fillets
1/4 tsp. sweet basil
2 Tbsp. Parmesan cheese
1/4 tsp. oregano
3 or 4 sliced mushrooms
juice of 1/2 fresh lime

1/8 tsp. garlic powder
2 Tbsp. bread crumbs
green pepper rings
2 Tbsp. butter
salt and pepper

Preheat oven to 350 degrees. Place fillets in a greased baking dish. Sprinkle with fresh lime juice, garlic powder, sweet basil and Parmesan cheese. Place one green pepper ring and a mushroom slice on top of each fillet. Sprinkle with salt and pepper. Cover each fillet with a light layer of bread crumbs and dribble butter across all the fillets. Bake for 20-30 minutes.

Sweet Potato Smelt

1 lb. smelt	1/2 tsp. salt
5 Tbsp. butter	1/8 tsp. pepper
5 Tbsp. lemon juice	1 cup cream
4 medium sweet potatoes	bread crumbs

Preheat oven to 425 degrees. Boil smelt until bones and skin can be removed easily. Mash. Add 1 tablespoon butter and 3 tablespoons lemon juice. Cook the sweet potatoes, drain and mash. Add pepper, 2 tablespoons lemon juice, salt and cream. blend with the mashed fish. If the mixture is too thick and dry, add a little milk. Place in baking dish, cover with crumbs and dot with remaining butter. Bake for 20 minutes.

Tangy Barbecued Fish

1 lb. frozen skinless	2 tsp. sugar
fish fillets, thawed	1 tsp. instant onions, minced
1/4 cup catsup	1/4 tsp. salt
3 Tbsp. lemon juice	dash of red pepper sauce
2 Tbsp. Worcestershire sauce	lemon wedges

Preheat oven to 400 degrees. Place fish fillets in ungreased baking dish (13" by 9" by 2"). Mix catsup, lemon juice, Worcestershire sauce, sugar, onion, salt and pepper sauce. Pour over fish; turn fish coating both sides. Cover and refrigerate 30 minutes. Bake uncovered for 15 to 20 minutes, until fish flakes easily with fork. Garnish with lemon wedges.

Tomato Baked Lake Trout

4 lbs. fillets	salt and pepper
2 onions, diced	1/4 cup water
1 1/2 cups corn flakes	1 tsp. butter
4 tomatoes, chopped	

Preheat oven to 350 degrees. Season fillets with salt and pepper. Place in greased baking dish. Mix together: onions, corn flakes, tomato and water. Pour over fish, add butter and sprinkle with paprika. Bake for 30 minutes.

Trout Stuffed with Crabmeat

4 whole trout
3 cups bread crumbs
1 cup milk
1 egg
1 egg yolk
1/3 cup raw bacon, chopped
1/3 cup onion, chopped

3 ozs. crabmeat
1/4 tsp. parsley
1/4 tsp. oregano
1 Tbsp. lemon juice
1/4 tsp. Worcestershire sauce
1/8 tsp. hot sauce
salt & pepper to taste

Without separating halves, split and debone trout. Soak bread crumbs in milk, squeeze dry add eggs. Saute bacon and onions. Add crabmeat and saute for 5 minutes. Add bread mixture, and mix in rest of ingredients. Spread stuffing on 1/2 of each trout. Fold over other half. Brush with melted butter, sprinkle with paprika. Bake in 400 degree oven 20—25 minutes until skin is brown and crisp.

Trout Stuffed With Crawdad Meat

2 (12" ea.) trout
4 ozs. cooked crawdad tails
  shelled, deveined, diced
1/2 stalk celery, diced
1/2 cup onion, diced
4 small mushrooms, sliced
1 Tbsp. butter

2 slices bread, toasted and
  cubed
dash pepper
dash salt
dash garlic
dash basil
1 egg

Preheat oven to 350 degrees. Melt butter in saucepan and saute onion, celery and mushrooms. Add bread cubes, crawdad meat, and seasonings. Cool. Add egg and mix well. Stuff trout carefully. Place the trout in a greased baking pan and bake for about 20 minutes, until fish flakes easily.

Trout with Shrimp & Crab

3 lbs. fillet of trout
24 shrimp, cooked
1/4 lb. mushrooms, sauted

1/4 lb. crabmeat
3 Tbsp. olive oil

Place trout in baking dish, sprinkle tip with oil. Bake at 375 degrees for 1/2 hour. While baking, mix sauce:

1/2 lb. butter, melted
2 Tbsp. lemon juice
1/4 tsp. salt

4 egg yolks
1/4 tsp. cayenne pepper
1 Tbsp. flour

Mix in blender on low speed, the egg yolks, lemon juice, salt and cayenne. Add warm melted butter and continue beating at low. Turn off, add flour, turn back on to blend in flour. Put sauce in the top of a double boiler over simmering water, add shrimp, undrained mushrooms, and the crabmeat. Stir. Place fish on warm platter, cover with hot sauce and serve. Serves 6.

Vegetable Stuffed Salmon

8 to 10 lb. salmon
salt and pepper
1 lemon
1 cup white wine

2 onions, cut into thick rings
2 tomatoes, cut into thick
  rings
2 oranges, cut into thick rings

Preheat oven to 350 degrees. Rub the inside cavity of salmon with salt, pepper, juice of the lemon and 1/4 cup of the wine. then stuff with the onion, tomato and orange slices, layered. Tie the fish together with thread and place it in a large baking dish or roasting pan. Pour in the remaining wine. Bake for about 50 minutes, or until the fish flakes easily. Baste occasionally so skin doesn't dry out. When done, remove thread and discard orange slices. Keep vegetable stuffing.

Walleye and Mushrooms

4 walleye fillets
2 Tbsp. dry white wine
1 can (2 oz.) mushrooms,
  chopped, with liquid

1/2 cup heavy cream
2 tsp. cornstarch
1/4 tsp. salt

Preheat oven to 325 degrees. Arrange fillets in greased baking dish. Sprinkle with white wine. Blend mushrooms (with liquid), cream, cornstarch and salt. Pour over fish and bake for 20 minutes or until fish flakes easily with a fork. Baste frequently.

Walleye Fillets with Parmesan Cheese

3 lbs. walleye fillets
2 cups fresh bread crumbs
  (use any soft white bread,
  trim crusts)

1 cup sour cream
2/3 cup parmesan cheese,
  grated
1 1/4 tsp. garlic salt

Preheat oven to 450 degrees. Combine bread crumbs, sour cream, Parmesan cheese and garlic salt in a mixing bowl or food processor. Wash and dry fish and place it in a buttered 9″ by 13″ baking dish. Spread bread crumb-cheese mixture over the fish. Bake for 15—20 minutes until fish flakes easily with a fork. Place the dish under the broiler a few minutes to brown.

Walleye in Butter Sauce

2 lbs. walleye fillets
1/4 cup butter
1 Tbsp. Worcestershire sauce
1/4 cup green onions,
  including tops, chopped

2 tsp .lemon juice
salt to taste
1 clove garlic, minced
1/4 tsp. cayenne pepper

Preheat oven to 375 degrees. Wash and dry fillets, and place in a baking dish. Combine all other ingredients and heat to boiling in a saucepan. Pour over the fish and bake for 35—40 minutes, or until fish flakes easily.

Walleye Parmesan

12 medium size fillets
1/2 cup tomato sauce
2 pkgs. (3/4 oz. ea.) garlic
  cheese salad mix

2 Tbsp. melted fat
2 Tbsp. chopped parsley
2 Tbsp. grated Parmesan cheese

Preheat oven to 350 degrees. Clean, wash and dry fish. Combine remaining ingredients except cheese. Brush fillets inside and out with tomato sauce. Place in a well greased baking dish (14"x9"x2"). Brush with remaining sauce and sprinkle with cheese. Let stand for 30 minutes. Bake 25—30 minutes until fish is fork tender. Turn over control to broil. Place fish about 3 inches below broiler and broil for 1—2 minutes or until crisp and lightly browned.

Walleye Pie

1 walleye fillet (1 1/2—2 lbs.)
  cut into bite-size pieces
1/2 cup butter
1/2 cup celery, chopped
1 small onion, chopped
1 1/2 cups milk
1/4 cup flour

1/2 cup white wine
3/4 cup Swiss cheese, grated
3 eggs
paprika
1 (9 inch) dish pie shell,
  unbaked

Preheat oven to 350 degrees. Melt butter in pan, add chopped celery, onion. Blend in flour, salt and pepper. Add milk all at once. Increase heat and cook quickly, stirring constantly until mixture thickens. Add wine and cheese, stirring until cheese melts; add walleye and bring to simmer. Beat eggs until lemon color and stir into fish mixture. Pour into pie shell and sprinkle with paprika. Bake for 45 minutes and let stand 10 minutes before serving.

Walleye Quiche

4 or 5 walleye fillets,
  poached and flaked
1 cup sharp American cheese
  cut into small cubes
1 pkg. (3 oz.) cream cheese
  cut into small cubes
1/4 cup green onions
  thinly sliced

1 cup spinach, chopped
1/2 cup mushrooms, sliced
2 cups milk
1 cup pancake mix
4 eggs
1/2 tsp. salt
1/2 tsp. pepper
1 tsp. dried parsley

Preheat oven to 400 degrees. Mix walleye, cheese, onions, spinach and mushrooms; place in a greased pie plate. Beat the remaining ingredients until smooth. Pour over the walleye mixture and bake about 35 minutes or until a knife inserted in the center comes out clean. Let stand about 5 minutes before serving.

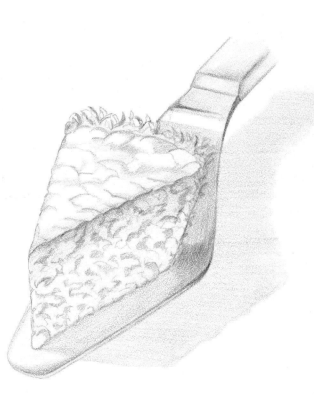

Walleye with Special Vegetable Sauce

2 lbs. walleye fillets
juice of 1 lemon

1/2 tsp. thyme
freshly ground pepper

For Sauce:

1 Tbsp. unsalted butter
1 Tbsp. sunflower or
  sunflower oil
2 large onions, sliced in rings
1 tsp. garlic, coarsely chopped
1 large green pepper, cut in
  thin strips

3 cups ripe tomatoes
2 Tbsp. dried basil, or 1 tsp.
  fresh basil, finely chopped
1/4 tsp. thyme
1/4 tsp. oregano
3/4 tsp. sugar
1/4 tsp. ground pepper

Preheat oven to 350 degrees. For topping: minced garlic, basil, oregano, and unsalted butter.

Lay fish out; sprinkle on all sides with lemon juice, thyme and ground pepper. Refrigerate.

Heat butter and oil in large skillet. Add onions. Cook about 10 minutes, separating rings as they cook. Add garlic and green pepper. Continue cooking and stirring until pepper strips are limp. Add tomatoes, basil, thyme, oregano, sugar, and grind of pepper. Cook, stirring well, for 5 minutes. Cover and cook gently for 30 minutes. Cool briefly.

Take fish from refrigerator; spoon 1 tablespoon vegetable sauce onto center of each fillet. Roll the fillets. Put remaining sauce in baking dish. Arrange fish rolls on top. Dot tops of each with equal amounts of finely-minced garlic, finely-chopped basil, crushed oregano and unsalted butter. Bake for 20—25 minutes, basting frequently.

BOILING

Boiled Fish A La Carte

2 - 3 lbs. fish fillets	4 - 6 bay leaves
4 qts. water	3 - 4 shakes hot sauce
2 Tbsp. salt	1 lemon, sliced thin

Heat above ingredients except fish to full boil in large pan. Cut fish into 2x4 inch pieces and add to pan. Cook until tender. Do not over cook. Remove fish from pan. Place on warm platter and serve with lemon slices and parsley. Spread hot lemon butter over fish and sprinkle with paprika.

Boiled Pike and Egg Sauce

3 lbs. pike	1 cup hot fish stock
1 Tbsp. butter	1 egg yolk, beaten
1 Tbsp. flour	

Clean fish and boil in salted water for 30 minutes. Reserve 1 cup fish stock. Melt butter, add flour and hot fish stock. Remove from heat and add egg yolk. Mix well. Pour over fish and garnish with parsley.

Catfish in Beer Sauce

12 small catfish	salt and pepper
beer	2 egg yolks, beaten

Clean fish and remove skin. Place in Dutch oven. Pour just enough beer to cover fish. Season with salt and pepper. Simmer until tender. Remove fish from pan and place on hot dish. Add egg yolks to the beer the fish were cooked in, stirring until smooth and thick. Pour over fish and serve.

Classy Bass

1 lb. bass fillets	1 tsp. dry mustard
water	1 Tbsp. Worcestershire sauce
1 tsp. vinegar	1/2 tsp. paprika
1 1/2 Tbsp. butter	1/2 tsp. salt
1 1/2 Tbsp. flour	3 Tbsp. dry sherry
3 cups hot milk	

Boil bass fillets in water with vinegar until fish flakes easily. Drain and flake fish. Blend butter and flour into smooth paste; cook and stir while slowly adding milk. Add bass flakes, dry mustard, Worcestershire sauce, paprika and salt. Simmer 5 minutes and add sherry.

Fish Vegetable Boil

4 lbs. fish steaks	5 onions, chopped
6 potatoes, quartered	drawn butter
6 carrots, sliced	parsley
3/4 cup salt	lemon

Fill Dutch oven with 5 quarts of water. Fill basket with potatoes and carrots and place into kettle; turn on high. When water comes to a full boil, slowly add 3/4 cup salt. Cook 10 minutes. Add onions, cook for another 10 minutes. Regulate heat to keep a full boil going continuously. Failure to do this will result in a salty-tasting fish boil. Place fish steaks into kettle. If boiling action subsides when the fish are first placed in the kettle, turn the heat up to quickly get the water boiling again. When the water comes to a full boil, cook fish another 12-15 minutes. Time may vary 2-3 minutes depending upon the amount of fish in kettle. Cook fish only until it can be flaked easily with a fork. Soft, mushy fish will result if fish are over cooked. Drain. Serve with hot drawn butter over fish and vegetables. Add parsley and lemon as a garnish.

Fish with Frosty Green Grapes

3 lbs. pike or trout
1/4 cup sugar
1 lemon
2 egg yolks, beaten
salt to taste

1 cup hot fish stock
1 tsp. chopped parsley
1 cup chilled seedless
green grapes

Boil fish until tender. Remove skin and bones and arrange fish on platter. Combine sugar, grated lemon rind and lemon juice with egg yolks, gradually add strained fish stock. Cook until thick, stirring constantly. Add salt and parsley. Pour over fish, garnish with grapes and serve immediately.

New England Style Pike

1 1/2 lb. northern pike
1 lb. cabbage, quartered
4 potatoes, cubed
4 carrots, cubed
1 onion, chopped
2 tsp. salt

3 Tbsp. butter
1 cup boiling water
few dashes red pepper
1 cup fresh, frozen or
canned peas

Saute onion in butter in large pan until soft. Add vegetables, arranging cabbage and peas on top, add salt, water and pepper; cover and simmer 10 minutes. Remove about half the cabbage and peas. Cut fish into serving size portions and place skin side down over vegetables. Cover with cabbage and peas. Cover pan tightly, simmer 5-10 minutes, until fish is tender. Drain liquid and add enough boiling water to make 1 cup. Blend 1 1/2 tablespoons flour with 3 tablespoons cold water to make a smooth paste; add to hot broth, cook stirring constantly until sauce thickens. Stir in 2 teaspoons lemon juice. Place fish and vegetables on hot platter, pour sauce over all, and sprinkle with 1 tablespoon parsley.

Stuffed Boiled Fish

1 fish
2 onions
1/4 cup cracker crumbs
1 egg, slightly beaten

1 tsp. salt
1/8 tsp. pepper
1 cup water
1/4 cup minced celery

Starting at back bone, remove all skin from fish in one piece. Remove bones and grind fillets. Grind onions. Combine 1/3 of onions with fish and grind again. Add cracker crumbs, egg, salt, pepper and water to fish. Mix until smooth. Wash fish skin thoroughly, fill with mixture and sew or skewer together. Place in kettle, add celery and remaining onions. Cover with boiling water and boil 5 minutes. Reduce heat and simmer 1 hour, adding water if necessary to prevent fish from burning.

Tasty Boiled Bass

2 lbs. bass fillets
1 cup parsley, finely chopped
1 onion, chopped fine

1 clove garlic, finely
chopped
salt and pepper to taste

Cut fish into slices 1 inch thick and place in skillet. Barley cover fish with water. Add remaining ingredients. Cover pan and simmer about 20 minutes until fish are done. Remove fish to platter and serve with melted butter.

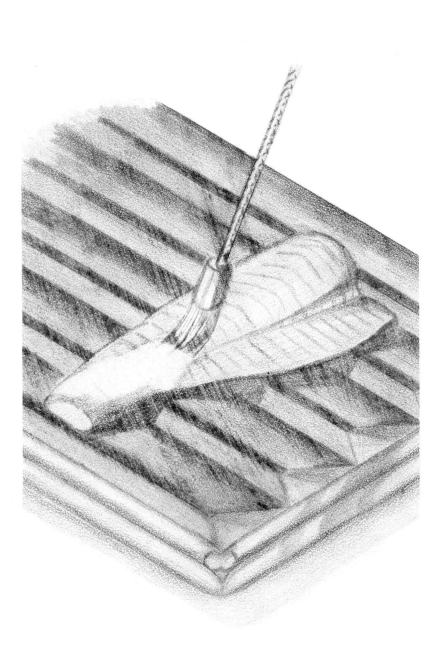

BROILING

Broiled Fillet of Fish

trout, perch or bass fillets
1 cup melted butter
1 tsp. parsley, chopped

paprika
1/2 cup lemon juice
salt and pepper

Clean fish well. Season fish with salt, pepper, and paprika. Rub fish with butter and place on broiler rack. Baste often with mixture of butter, lemon juice, and parsley. Broil each side 10-15 minutes, depending on size of fillets. Meat is done when it falls away from fork easily. Garnish with lemon wedges and parsley. Serve with lemon butter or tartar sauce.

Broiled Fish Fillets with Cheese Sauce

2 lbs. cod fillets
3 cups soft, grated bread crumbs

salad or olive oil
Cheese Sauce

Cut cod fillets into serving size pieces. Brush on both sides with oil; dredge in bread crumbs. Broil at 350 degrees for 15 minutes, turning once. Serve with Cheese Sauce.

Cheese Sauce:

2 cups diced American cheese 2 tsp. paprika 2 tsp. dry mustard 4 tsp. Worcestershire sauce 1 cup Budweiser Beer

Combine ingredients; cook over low heat, stirring occasionally, until cheese melts and mixture is smooth.

Broiled Flounder

2 lbs. flounder   3 Tbsp. oil
3 Tbsp. lemon juice   salt and pepper to taste
parsley sprigs and lemon wedges for garnish

Rinse fish in cold water and pat dry. Brush broiler rack with oil and arrange fish on it. Combine oil and lemon juice in small bowl and brush over fish. Salt and pepper to taste. Place fish 4 inches under the broiler unit and broil for 5-8 minutes , or until fish flakes easily when tested with fork but is suntil moist. Remove fish and garnish with parsley and lemon wedges.

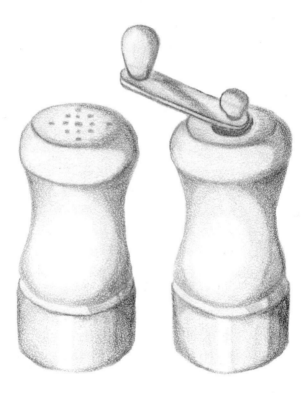

Broiled Lake Trout

1 large lake trout
1-2 Tbsp. olive oil
lemon butter

1 garlic clove
1/4 tsp. white pepper
parsley for garnish

Preheat broiler. Rub a small bowl with the garlic; add olive oil and white pepper to same bowl. Coat fish with oil mixture. Place fish in greased, shallow pan. Broil until brown, turning once. Spread fish with lemon butter and garnish with parsley.

Broiled Mackerel

1 mackerel (2—3 lbs.) fresh
  or frozen
3-4 green onions, chopped
1/2 tsp. dry mustard
1/4 tsp. cayenne pepper

1/2 stick butter
2 Tbsp. parsley, chopped
2 Tbsp. lemon juice or vinegar
1/2 tsp. salt

Soak mackerel in cold water in a large covered bowl and place in refrigerator for several hours or overnight. Drain before cooking. Dry fish and remove fins. In a broiler pan, Saute green onions and parsley in hot butter until onions are soft. Place mackerel into pan, roll in hot butter until thoroughly coated. Place under broiler so fish are about 3 inches from the source of heat. Broil approximately 10 minutes, basting several times with melted butter. After first 5 minutes of broiling, sprinkle fish with salt and cayenne pepper and turn. Fish are done when flaked easily with a fork.

Broiled Salmon Steaks

4 salmon steaks
4 Tbsp. French salad dressing
2 Tbsp. soy sauce

1/2 tsp. ground ginger
1 lemon, sliced thin

Combine salad dressing, soy sauce, and ginger. Place fish on a cookie sheet. Brush both sides of fish with sauce and let stand for 10 minutes. Broil for 8 minutes, then turn fish. Brush with any remaining sauce and broil on second side for 5 minutes, or until fish flakes when tested with a fork. Garnish with lemon slices.

Buttered Lake Trout

4 (8 oz.) trout fillets
1/2 cup soft butter
1/2 clove garlic, minced fine
salt and pepper to taste
4 Tbsp. melted butter

2 Tbsp. white wine
1 green onion, diced fine
dash cayenne
paprika

Brush fillets with melted plain butter. Season with salt and pepper. Sprinkle with paprika. Place fish under broiler, turning once. Broil until fish flakes easily. Remove from heat and top with sauce.

Sauce:

To 1/2 cup soft butter, add white wine, garlic, green onion and cayenne. Mix thoroughly. Let stand for 15 minutes before using. (This butter may be refrigerated for an extended period of time.)

Catfish Mexican Style

2 lbs. catfish fillets   1 Tbsp. horseradish
1/4 cup chili sauce   1/4 cup apricot jam
2 Tbsp. mustard

Mix chili sauce, mustard, horseradish and jam. Brush on fillets. Place fish on rack and broil about 5 minutes, turn and broil another 5 minutes.

Lake Trout Divine

six 1 inch trout steaks   1 Tbsp. lemon juice
1/3 cup butter, melted   paprika
salt and pepper

Place fish steaks on greased broiler pan and brush with melted butter, lemon juice, and seasonings. Broil about 2 inches from heat for 7 minutes. Turn fish and brush other side. Broil 3 minutes longer or until fish flakes easily.

Sesame Seed Bass Fillets

bass fillets
1 Tbsp. lemon juice
1 Tbsp. sesame seeds

1/2 cup melted butter
1/4 tsp. parsley flakes

Place fillets on a lightly greased broiler pan. Baste with mixture of lemon juice, melted butter and parsley. Place broiler pan about 4 inches from the heat source and broil for about 3-4 minutes on the first side. Carefully turn fillets and broil for additional 2-3 minutes. Remove and sprinkle lightly with sesame seeds.

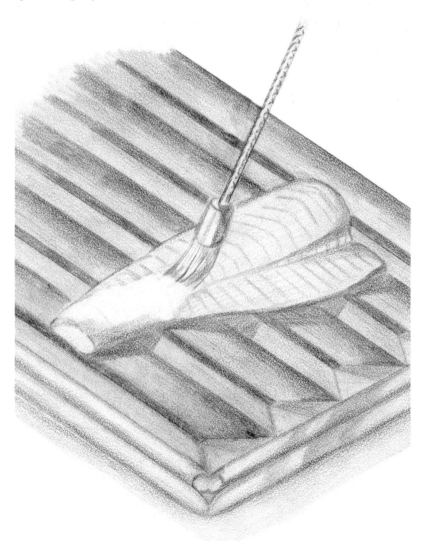

Sweet-and-Sour Fillets

1 1/2 lbs. fillets
1/4 cup soy sauce
2 Tbsp. cooking oil
1 1/2 tsp. lemon juice
1/4 tsp. pepper
2 Tbsp. parsley, chopped

1/4 cup orange juice
1 small tomato, seeded and
  chopped
1/4 tsp. oregano
1 clove garlic, chopped fine

Place fillets in a baking dish. Combine ingredients and pour over fish. Marinade for 1 hour, turning once. Place fillets on a buttered sheet of aluminum foil in a broiler pan. Broil 4 inches from heat 5 minutes per side. As you turn fish over, pour a small amount of the marinade on each fillet. Serve immediately on heated platter.

Tangy Crappie Fillets

6 large crappie fillets
1/2 lb. butter, melted
juice of 6 limes
salt and pepper

12 raw shrimp (peeled
  deveined, minced)
black pepper, milled

Mix 3/4 cup butter, juice of 4 limes, shrimp, and pepper. Blend well. Place fillets on broiler, spoon sauce over fish and broil for 12 minutes, basting with sauce often. Sprinkle hot lime juice over hot plates, place fish on plates, brush with hot melted butter and sprinkle with salt and pepper to taste.

Tasty Salmon Steaks with Herb Sauce

6 (2 lb.) coho salmon steaks
1/4 cup dry white wine
1/4 tsp. finest herbs blend
1 tsp. salt

1/4 cup butter or margarine
1 Tbsp. chopped parsley
1 clove garlic sliced

Combine butter or margarine, wine, parsley, herbs and garlic; heat slowly until fat is melted. Let stand 15 minutes. Sprinkle steaks with salt. Place fish on well greased broiler pan; brush with sauce. Broil about 3 inches from heat source, 4—6 minutes. Turn carefully, brush with sauce. Broil 4—6 minutes longer or until fish flakes easily when tested with a fork.

Baste steaks with sauce several times while broiling. Serve with lemon wedges. Serves 6.

Vermouth Perch

6 large perch fillets
1/2 cup dry vermouth
1 cup butter, melted

3 Tbsp. fine bread crumbs
2 Tbsp. cheese, grated

Mix butter and vermouth and pour half over the perch in shallow baking dish. Broil fish for 8 minutes. Sprinkle with bread crumbs and cheese and broil for another 4 minutes, basting constantly with the remaining butter vermouth mixture.

CANNING, PICKLING & SMOKING

Canned Fish

Duel Delight

fish, cleaned
1 tsp. oil
1 Tbsp. vinegar

1/4 cup tomato sauce
1 tsp. canning salt

Cut fish in small pieces. Pack in pint jars and pour sauce over fish. Cook mixture for 80 minutes at 10 pounds of pressure. To make a dip: mix some of the canned fish, with 2 tablespoons of salad dressing, diced onions and 1/8 teaspoon of celery seed, or fresh celery.

From Smelt to Sardines

1 pt. smelt, cleaned
3 Tbsp. vinegar

2 Tbsp. cooking oil
1 Tbsp. salt

Combine all ingredients together and place in pint jars, seal. Cook mixture in pressure cooker at 10 pounds of pressure for 80 minutes.

Never Fail Tidbits

2 cups fish, cut-up (bite size)
1 Tbsp. catsup
1/2 Tbsp. salt

1 Tbsp. cooking oil
1 Tbsp. vinegar

Combine all of the above ingredients and place in a pint jar. Process in pressure cooker at 10 pounds pressure for 90 minutes. Makes 1 pint.

Sealed Sucker

1 qt. fish, cleaned
1 tsp. salt
1 tsp. dry mustard
1/8 tsp. pepper

1/8 tsp. garlic
6 Tbsp. vinegar
3 Tbsp. catsup

Add all ingredients to fish in quart jar. Put 2 more teaspoons of catsup on top. Seal jars loosely and boil 6 hours in canner. Tightly seal jars. Let stand 3 months.

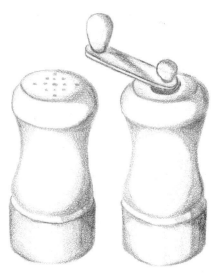

Snappy Snack

fish
1 tsp. salt
1/4 cup vinegar

1 tsp. brown sugar
1/4 cup tomato cocktail juice

Pack chunks of raw fish into pint jars. Mix together above ingredients. Pour over fish in jars, seal. Pressure at 10 pounds for 90 minutes.

Tomato Wonder

fish, cut into 2-3" chunks
1 1/2 Tbsp. vinegar
1 Tbsp. tomato soup
1 tsp. salt

few drops red food coloring
onion slices
2 Tbsp. catsup

Place ingredients into pint jar and pack tightly with fish chunks. Cook by cold pack method 4 hours or in a pressure cooker at 15 pounds. for 90 minutes.

Pickled Fish

Almost Forgotten Pickling Solution

2 cups white vinegar
5 medium white onions, sliced
5 lemons, sliced
2 tsp. mustard seed
1 3/4 cups sugar
4 bay leaves

5 whole cloves
1 tsp. whole allspice
1 tsp. whole black peppercorns
5—6 red peppers
few drops hot sauce

Mix all ingredients together and bring pickling solution to a boil, then cool. Remove fish from brine solution and place in clean gallon container. Add pickling solution to cover fish. If more solution is needed, add white wine (Rhine or Sauterne). Cover and refrigerate a minimum of 1 week before using. The longer it sits the better it tastes.

Easy-Does-It Pickled Fish

4 lbs. fish   1 cup vinegar
salt   2 Tbsp. mixed pickling spices
2 onions, sliced   1 Tbsp. sugar
1 qt. water

Clean fish without removing skin or bones. Slice and season with salt. Cook onions in water for 20 minutes. Add vinegar, whole spices tied in cheesecloth bag, sugar, lemon and fish. Boil for 1 hour. Remove fish, cut in smaller portions. Strain liquid and pour over fish. Store with liquid in canning jar. Serves about 6.

One Day Delight

4 lbs. oily fish   1 pt. white vinegar
16 oz. lime juice   6 bay leaves
2 onions, sliced thin   1 tomato, diced
whole peppercorns   1/2 tsp. red pepper
1/8 tsp. hot sauce   (ground)
1/8 tsp. parsley flakes   salt and pepper
2 Tbsp. olive oil   1/8 tsp. dry mustard
whole little red pepper

Mix above ingredients in crock bowl, stirring occasionally. You may have to add more salt after it stands awhile. You will be able to tell by taste. Will be ready to eat after 24 hours. Keeps in refrigerator for a week. When fish gets low you may add more fish, making sure all fish are under the liquid.

Pickled Fish-1

fish fillets   7 Tbsp. sugar
2 Tbsp. salt   1 1/2 oz. dry white wine
2 tsp. whole mixed pickling spice   apple cider vinegar

Fillet and skin fish. Be sure to remove the rib cages. Now cut them into about 1 1/2-inch-square chunks or 1/4- to 1-inch strips. Fill a quart jar 3/4 full of fillets plus 1 diced onion. Pack very loosely. Add the following.

Fill the jar with wine and vinegar. Now shake the jar to thoroughly mix the ingredients. Refrigerate for four days. During the four days shake the jar from time to time.

Pickled Fish-2

2 qts. cubed fish
2 qts. cold water
1 cup pickling salt

1 1/2 cups sugar
3 medium onions, sliced
3 tsp. pickling spices

Put the fish, cold water, and pickling salt in a gallon earthen or glass jar and place in the refrigerator for 48 hours. Then wash fish real well in cold water. Cut in bite-sized pieces, wash again and dry on paper towels. Then put the sugar, onions, and spices in the gallon jar.

Add fish and cover with white vinegar. Place in the refrigerator for 48 hours. The fish is now ready to eat, you can put it in smaller jars if you would like. Keep refrigerated.

Pickled Fish-3

fish
3 Tbsp. salt
1/4 cup sugar

white vinegar
1 medium diced onion
2 tsp. pickling spice

Fillet and cut strips into 1-inch wide strips. Fill quart jar 3/4 full with fish strips. Add salt, sugar, spice and onion, fill remainder of jar with white vinegar. Cover and refrigerate. Ready to eat in 4 days.

(You only have to remove large bones, as the small ones will dissolve.)

Pickled Fish-4

1 lb. cut up fish	1/2 cup white sherry
5/8 cup pickling salt	2 Tbsp. pickling spice
2 cups white vinegar	1 cup sugar

Place fish in pickling salt mixed with 1 cup of white vinegar. Leave in refrigerator for five days. Stir gently once daily to mix brine. This should dissolve big bones.

Wash fish in cold water until clear. Soak for 1 hour in cold water. Heat but do not boil 1 cup of white vinegar, sugar, white sherry, and pickling spice. Spices should be bagged and remain in the solution until it has cooled to room temperature.

Place alternate layers of fish and onion slices in jars. Add a pinch of spices and fill jars with above solution. Seal jars and refrigerate for three days before tasting.

Pickled Fish-5

4 cups white vinegar	1/2 cup sugar
1 cup water	1 Tbsp. mixed pickling spices

Make a brine of water and salt; 2 cups of salt to 1 gallon of water. Have fish skinned and cut into small pieces. Soak fish pieces in this brine for 24 hours. Rinse off quickly in cold, fresh water. Pour off right away.

Heat the vinegar, water, sugar, and pickling spices. You can also add sliced lemon and onion. Ready the following day.

Pickled Salmon

2 lbs. of salmon   1/4 tsp. bay leaves
3/4 cup + 2 Tbsp. disuntiled vine-
gar   3/4 cup + 2 Tbsp. water
5 tsp. olive oil   3 1/2 Tbsp. sliced onions
1/2 tsp. white peppers   1/2 tsp. mustard seed
1/4 tsp. cloves   1/4 tsp. black peppers

Cut 2 pounds of salmon into individual serving portions. Wash well in cold water, drain, and dredge in fine salt. After 1/2 hour, rinse off salt, and simmer the salmon until done. Place the warm fish in an earthenware crock, and cover with a vinegar spice sauce.

Cook the onions in olive oil slowly until yellow and soft. Add the rest of the ingredients and simmer gently for 45 minutes. Allow the sauce to cool, and pour over the fish, making sure all pieces are covered. Allow to stand 24 hours before using. This method may be used for mackerel, shad and other large fish.

Pike's Delight

3—4 cups northern
8 cups vinegar
5/8 cup salt

3 cups sugar
1/2 box of pickling spices
1 whole large onion, sliced

Skin and fillet fish, cut into bite size pieces (3 or 4 cups). Mix vinegar and salt. Pour over fish, and let stand in refrigerator one weekdrain fish. Soak 1 hour in cold water. Mix 4 cups vinegar with 3 cups sugar and 1/2 box pickling spices. Bring to boilthen cool. Put layers of fish and onions in a gallon jar, pour cooled brine to cover. Let stand in refrigerator three weeks.

Quick-and-Easy Pickled Fish

raw fish
4 cups white vinegar
4 cups cold water
2 large onions, sliced thin

1/2 cup salt
1 1/2 cups sugar
3 Tbsp. pickling spice

Combine mixture and pour into a 1 gallon glass jar. Fill to top with thin sliced raw fish. Let stand at room temperature for 48 hours with lid on loosely. Pour off brine, leaving just enough to cover the fish. Keep in refrigerator indefinitely.

Suddenly Herring

5 lbs. fish, cut into herring
   size cubes
3 large onions, sliced thin
1 1/2 cups sugar

1 cup pickling salt
2 bay leaves
4 Tbsp. pickling spices
white vinegar

Cover fish with cold water. Add 1 cup pickling salt and refrigerate for 2 days. Rinse fish throughly and drain on paper towel. In crock or large jar, place fish, sugar, onion slices, pickling spices, and bay leaves. Cover with white vinegar and gently stir ingredients together. Refrigerate for another 2 days. Fish will now be ready to eat and you may divide into smaller jars, making sure each jar has onions and spices, and that the fish are covered with white vinegar.

Smoked Fish

Smoking Brine

1 qt. cold water
1/4 cup sugar
other seasoning to taste

1/3 cup non-iodized or
   kosher salt
1/2 tsp. pepper

Pour water in pan large enough to hold fish; add salt and sugar, stir to dissolve (brine should float an egg). Add seasonings. Add fish to brine; leaving 1 inch.

DEEP FRYING

Batter-Dipped Fish

2 lbs. fish fillets
2 eggs
2/3 cup milk
1 cup flour

1 tsp. baking powder
1/2 tsp. salt
2 Tbsp. melted shortening
oil

Beat milk and eggs together. Sift together flour, baking powder and salt; add to egg mixture. Add shortening and beat until blended. Dip fish into batter, allow excess batter to run off. Fry in hot oil until golden brown. Drain and serve.

Batter Smelt

15—20 smelt
1/4 cup flour
1 egg, beaten
1/4 cup cornstarch
1/4 cup beer

salt, pepper, and paprika
1/4 cup butter, melted
   and cooled
butter and shortening equal
   amounts

Clean and dry smelt. Combine flour, cornstarch and set aside. Mix beer and egg together. Add melted butter and gradually add the flour and cornstarch, making a smooth batter. Season smelt with salt, pepper and paprika. Dip smelt into batter and deep fry in hot oil until brown.

Black Crappie Cakes

2 lbs. crappie, flaked
2 eggs, beaten
1 cup milk
2 slices bread, crust removed
2 Tbsp. mayonnaise

1/2 tsp. salt
2 tsp. Worcestershire sauce
2 Tbsp. baking powder
2 tsp. seafood seasoning
1 tsp. celery seed

Cover fish with salted water and simmer until flaky. Moisten bread slices with milk. Combine all ingredients and mix thoroughly. Shape into small cakes. Deep fry at 375 degrees until brown.

Bucketmouth with Parmesan Cheese

3 lbs. fillets
1 1/4 cups flour
4 eggs

3 Tbsp. grated Parmesan
  cheese
4 Tbsp. flat beer

Combine cheese, flour, salt and eggs, beat well; add beer. Stir constantly. Roll fillets in flour then dip in batter. Allow excess batter to fall from fillets. Carefully lower fillets into hot oil and fry until golden brown.

Buttermilk Crisp Fillets

2 lbs. fish fillets
1 cup buttermilk
1 cup biscuit mix

salt and pepper
shortening

Soak fillets in buttermilk for 30 minutes. Drain, sprinkle with salt and pepper. Dip fish in biscuit mix. Deep fry in hot shortening at 375 degrees until brown and tender.

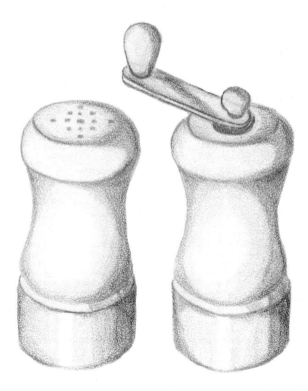

Cod Balls

1 cup flaked cooked cod
1 1/2 cups mashed potatoes
1 egg beaten
1 Tbsp. butter, melted

1/4 tsp. salt
1/8 tsp. pepper
1/2 tsp. onion juice

Mix all ingredients together and beat until smooth. Shape into balls or cakes. Fry in hot fat 375 degrees until browned.

Codfish Puffs: Use 2 eggs instead of 1. Beat mixture, and drop from spoon into hot oil.

Cod Batter Fried

2 lbs. fish fillets
2 cups flour
2 eggs
2 cups milk
1 onion, sliced thin

5 Tbsp. oil
4 Tbsp. white wine
4 Tbsp. lemon juice
salt
lemon pepper

Season fillets with salt and lemon pepper. Mix oil, white wine and lemon juice together. Marinate fish in mixture for 1 hour. Lay onion slices on fillets while marinating. Mix flour, eggs and milk for batter. Remove fillets after the hour and drain. Dip fillets into batter. Deep-fry in hot oil until well browned.

Crappie and Beer Deepfry

2 lbs. fillets
2 cups pancake flour
1 1/2 cups beer

2 eggs
1 tsp. salt
1/2 tsp. pepper

Combine beer, pancake flour, salt and pepper. Add beaten eggs and mix into a smooth batter. Dip fillets into batter, draining off excess batter. Carefully lower fillets into hot oil and cook until done, no more than 2 minutes.

Crispy Catfish

2 lbs. fillets
1 cup flour
1 cup beer

1/4 tsp. pepper
1/4 tsp. paprika
cooking oil

Mix flour, pepper and paprika. Slowly add beer until batter is smooth. Fry fish in 375 degree oil until golden brown.

Deep Fried Fillets

1 lb. fish fillets
1/2 cup flour
1/2 cup cornstarch
1/2 tsp. salt

1/4 tsp. dried marjoram,
    crushed
1 egg, separated
1/2 cup water

Combine dry ingredients together and mix. Beat egg yolk and water together and add to dry ingredients, mixing lightly. Beat egg whites until stiff, and fold into the batter. Dip fish into batter, then into hot oil and fry at 375 degrees until golden brown.

Deep Fried Panfish

1 lb. fillets
1 (12 oz.) can beer
1 cup flour
oil

1 tsp. salt
1 tsp. dill weed
1 Tbsp. paprika

Combine beer, flour, salt, dill weed and paprika. Mix together until smooth. Chill both batter and fish until ready to cook. Pat fish dry. Dip fish into batter. Lower into hot oil (375 degrees). Fry at until brown.

Deep Fried Pike

6 fillets
2 cups flour
2 eggs, separated
2 Tbsp. baking powder

2 tsp. salt
1 cup lukewarm water
2 Tbsp. shortening, melted

Rinse fillets and pat dry. Beat egg whites until they are stiff. Combine egg yolks, flour, salt and baking powder; mix with water and melted shortening. Beat and fold in egg whites. Dip fillets in batter, drain excess batter and lower into hot oil and fry at 375 degrees until brown.

Deep Fried Soaked Smelt

smelt
2 eggs
milk

3 Tbsp. rich cream
salt and pepper
sifted bread crumbs

Soak smelt in milk for 1/2 hour. Mix eggs, cream, salt, pepper and enough bread crumbs to make a smooth batter. Dip smelt into batter and deep fry until done.

Deep Fried Walleye

2 lbs. fillets
4 oz. saltine crackers
3 eggs

1/4 cup milk
salt and pepper

Combine eggs and milk; beat well. Sprinkle crushed crackers with salt and pepper. Dip fillets in egg mixture then cracker crumbs and deep fry in hot oil until golden brown. Drain on paper towel and serve.

Delicious Panfish

2 lbs. fillets
1 cup flour
1 egg, beaten
1/4 cup evaporated milk
1 cup crackers, finely crushed

1/4 tsp. salt
1/8 tsp. pepper
1/4 tsp. dried marjoram,
   crushed
1/4 tsp. dried thyme, crushed

Combine flour, salt and pepper. Mix egg and milk together. Now mix cracker crumbs and herbs together. Roll fillets in flour mixture, then egg mixture, then into cracker crumb mixture. Drop into hot oil and fry until golden brown.

Fillets Supreme

6 fillets
24 medium shrimp, cleaned
and deveined
2 Tbsp. parsley, chopped
6 green onions, finely
chopped (including tops)
1 clove garlic
1 bay leaf
1 1/2 cups dry white wine

1 Tbsp. butter
1 cup mushrooms, sliced
1 Tbsp. lemon juice
1 oz. dry white wine
1 oz. calvados, or applejack
salt and pepper
1 cup cream
1 egg yolk
2 Tbsp. butter

Place shrimp in pan over parsley, onions, garlic and bay leaf. Add white wine and butter. Cook over low heat for 10-15 minutes or until shrimp are done. Remove shrimp, reserving liquid. Boil mushrooms in enough water to half cover mushrooms (to which lemon juice has been added) for 3 minutes. Remove mushrooms and reserve liquid. In skillet, lightly saute mushrooms in butter. Remove mushrooms. Rinse skillet that mushrooms were sauted in with 1 ounce dry white wine and 1 ounce calvados or applejack. Into large skillet, strain liquid that shrimp were cooked in, and liquid and juices in which the mushrooms were cooked. Heat to boiling point, season with salt and pepper. Place fillets in the liquid and poach without boiling 10-15 minutes or until done. Remove fillets to hot serving dish, arrange shrimp and mushrooms around fillets and keep hot. Over high heat, reduce liquid in which fish were poached to about 1/2 cup. Let cool slightly and add 1 cup cream mixed with egg yolk and 2 tablespoons butter. Blend well over low heat until sauce is light and thickened slightly. Pour sauce over fillets, shrimps, and mushrooms. Serve.

Fish and Chips England Style

1 lb. fish fillets, cut into
   1 1/2 x 2" pieces
5 potatoes, cut lengthwise
2/3 cup flour
1/2 tsp. salt
1/2 tsp. baking soda

1 Tbsp. vinegar
2/3 cup water
malt or cider vinegar
vegetable oil
salt

Fill basket one-fourth full with potatoes; slowly lower into oil. Fry potatoes 5—7 minutes or until golden brown. Drain potatoes; place in single layer on cookie sheet. Combine flour and 1/2 teaspoon salt. Mix baking soda and 1 tablespoon vinegar with water. Stir vinegar and water mixture into flour, beat until smooth. Dip fish into batter, allow excess batter to drip off. Fry until brown. Broil potatoes 6 inches from heat until crisp. Sprinkle potatoes with vinegar and salt.

Fish Flake Crunch

2 cups flaked cooked fish
1 egg beaten
1 cup white sauce
1 tsp. onion juice

salt and pepper
parsley, chopped
cracker crumbs

Mix seasonings with fish flakes. Add white sauce and chill throughly. Shape into croquettes, roll in cracker crumbs, dip into egg and roll in crumbs again. Fry in deep hot oil until brown.

Fish Nuggets

1 lb. fish
3 eggs, separated
3 Tbsp. flour
1 Tbsp. parsley, minced

1/8 tsp. garlic, minced
1/2 tsp. salt
1/8 tsp. pepper

Remove skin and bones from cooked fish. Beat egg yolks until light and thick. Add flour, salt, pepper, garlic, parsley and fish. Fold in egg whites that have been beaten stiff. Drop by tablespoons into hot oil and fry until brown.

Fish Shake

1 1/2 cups pancake flour   1 tsp. salt
2 tsp. paprika   2 tsp. pepper

Clean fish and remove skin. Combine flour, paprika, salt and pepper in paper bag. Place fish in bag and shake until coated. Place fish in hot deep fat and fry until brown. Remove and drain on paper toweling.

Fried Fillets in Beer Batter

fish fillets   1/4 tsp. paprika
1 cup flour   1 egg, beaten
1 tsp. salt   1 cup beer
1/4 tsp. pepper

Mix dry ingredients together. Add egg and beer, stirring until smooth. Roll fillets in flour then dip in batter. Lower into hot oil and fry until golden brown.

Fried Fish Strips

1 lb. fillets
1 1/2 tsp. salt
1 tsp. baking powder
1/2 cup milk

1 cup flour
1 tsp. poultry seasoning
1 egg
1 Tbsp. salad oil

Sift dry ingredients together. Cut fillets into 1 x 2 1/2-inch strips. Roll fish strips in dry mixture. Beat egg and milk together to make 3/4 cup liquid. Add salad oil. Add liquid to remaining flour mixture and stir. Dip fish in batter. Fry in deep fat until golden brown.

Grandpa's Walleyes

4 walleye fillets
cooking oil
salt and pepper
3 cups flour
1 onion, chopped
2—3 Tbsp. flaked parsley

2 Tbsp. lemon juice
1/2 tsp. garlic salt
1/2 tsp. onion salt
2 cans beer
2 cups cornflakes

Heat 2-3 inches of oil to a high temperature, almost bubbling, in deep skillet or electric frying pan. Use enough oil so the fillets float. Salt and pepper the fillets.

Mix the flour and onion, add the parsley, lemon juice, garlic salt, and onion salt. Gradually stir in 1 can of beer. Crush cornflakes and add to the mixture. Beat to consistency of light pancake batter using as much of second can of beer as necessary. If batter thickens while standing, add more beer. If it gets too thin, add more crushed cornflakes.

Dip fillets in batter and drop gently into hot oil. Turn over when golden brown. This batter is also excellent for onion rings, mushrooms and cauliflower.

Hush Puppies Delight

fish fillets, cooked and flaked
2 cups white corn meal
1/4 cup green pepper, chopped fine

1 egg, beaten
3/4 cup milk
1 onion, chopped fine

Combine above ingredients together. Drop by large tablespoons into hot fat and fry until golden brown.

Hush Puppies with Creamed Corn

fish fillets, cooked and flaked
1 1/2 cup self-rising meal
1/2 cup flour
1 egg

1 onion, chopped
1 can (8 oz.) creamed corn
1/4 cup beer (room temp.)
1/4 tsp. garlic powder

Mix above ingredients together, adding more beer if mixture becomes to thick. Drop by pressed tablespoonfuls into hot oil. Fry until they float to top and turn over by themselves.

In-a-Rush Smelt

2 lbs. smelt
salt and pepper to taste

garlic salt, to taste

Drop cleaned smelt into hot oil for 2—4 minutes. Drain and sprinkle with seasoning. Serve.

Mustard Bass

bass fillets
prepared mustard
corn meal

salt
cooking oil

Cut fillets in half. Salt and apply mustard to each piece. Roll in corn meal and drop into hot oil. You may use other fish fry mixes, flour, or pancake mixes.

Opened Smelt

Clean smelt, removing the head and insides. Snip off fins. Place smelt, belly down, on a chopping board. With the palm of your hand, press down on the back of the fish until flat. Turn over. By starting at the back bone, you can lift the bones out whole. Deep fry using a beer batter, or spread with butter and broil for 5-8 minutes, or bake for 15 minutes at 450 degrees.

Perch Japanese Style

4 lbs. fillets
1 lemon, halved

1 qt. vegetable oil
Batter recipe (see below)

Cut fillets into bite-size pieces. Season with salt and drizzle with lemon juice.

Batter:

2 cups flour, sifted
3 egg yolks

2 cups ice water

Sift flour 3 times. Beat egg yolks and water in large bowl over ice until well blended. Gradually add flour, stirring and turning the mixture from the bottom with a spoon. Do not over mix, flour should be visible on top of batter. Keep the batter over ice while dipping and frying. Dip fish in batter, drain slightly, fry in deep hot fat until golden brown.

Porcupine Fish Balls

2 cups fish, cooked
2 cups rice, cooked
2 eggs, beaten
1/2 tsp. salt
1/8 tsp. paprika

1 Tbsp. lemon juice
1 tsp. onion, grated
2 Tbsp. parsley, chopped
crushed cornflakes

Combine flaked fish with rice, eggs, salt, paprika, lemon juice, onion and parsley. Stir until well blended. Roll into balls. Roll in cornflake crumbs, coating well. Deep fry in hot shortening until brown. Drain and serve.

Potato and Fish Puffs

1 lb. boneless fillets
5 potatoes, quartered
2 eggs

1/2 cup milk
2 Tbsp. onion, chopped fine
salt and pepper

Place potatoes and fish in cold water and cover. Bring to boil and cook until potatoes are done. Drain. Mash potatoes and fish together thoroughly. Mix eggs and milk together; combine with fish potato mixture. Mix thoroughly. Form into balls and deep fry.

Quick-and-Easy Fillets

1 lb. fish fillets
1 egg, beaten
1/2 cup flour
salt and pepper

oil
1 Tbsp. water
fine bread crumbs

Season fish with salt and pepper. Mix egg with water. Dip fish in flour then in egg mixture and roll in bread crumbs. Lower fish into hot oil. Fry until golden brown. Drain well and serve.

Sesame Seed Smelt

2 lbs. smelt, cleaned
1 1/2 tsp. salt
1/8 tsp. pepper
1 cup pancake mix

1/4 cup yellow cornmeal
1 1/4 cup milk
1 jar sesame seeds
1/2 cup flour

Sprinkle both inside and outside of fish with salt and pepper. Combine pancake mix, cornmeal and milk; stir until blended. Add sesame seeds. Roll fish in flour and dip in batter. Place in single layer in fry basket. Deep fry until brown. Drain and serve.

Smelt Fry

4 lbs. smelt
8 Tbsp. lemon juice

1 cup cream
1 cup flour

Clean smelt, removing heads and tails. Season with lemon juice and let stand for 1 hour in refrigerator. Dip smelt into cream and roll in flour. Lower into hot oil and cook until brown, about 4—5 minutes.

160

Stuffed Fish Rolls

4 fish fillets, (1 1/2 lbs.)
2 slices boiled ham
1 egg
1/4 cup chopped onion
1 Tbsp. soy sauce
1 tsp. cornstarch

1 tsp. grated gingerroot
1/2 tsp. sugar
1/8 tsp. pepper
1/2 cup finely chopped
   fresh spinach

Thaw fish, if frozen. Skin fillets, if necessary. Cut fish into eight 3 x 2 inch pieces. Cut slices of ham into quarters. In a shallow bowl combine egg, onion, soy sauce, cornstarch, gingerroot, sugar, and pepper; mix well. Dip fish pieces into egg mixture. Place one piece of ham on each fish piece. Spread 1 tablespoon of spinach over ham. Fold fish over to enclose filling. Secure with wooden picks.

Fry fish rolls, a few at a time, in deep hot oil (365 degrees) for 2 to 3 minutes or until golden. Using slotted spoon or wire strainer remove and drain on paper towel. Keep warm while frying remaining fish rolls.

Tangy Fish Marinated

2 lbs. fish fillets
1/4 cup ketchup
1 tsp. Worcestershire sauce
1/3 cup tomato juice
1/8 tsp. pepper

1/4 cup onion, chopped
1 Tbsp. vinegar
3 Tbsp. lemon juice
1/2 tsp. celery salt
dry bread crumbs

Mix onion, ketchup, vinegar, Worcestershire, lemon juice, tomato juice and seasonings. Cook for 5 minutes. Cool, pour over fish. Cover and marinate several hours in refrigerator. Remove fish, drain and roll in bread crumbs. Fry in hot oil until done.

Tasty Sticks

3 lbs. fillets
1 egg, beaten well

1 cup flour
1 cup cornmeal

Remove all bones and skin from cleaned fish. Cut fillets into sticks 2 inches long and 1 inch wide. Dip into egg, roll into cornmeal and flour mix. Fry in hot fat. Salt and pepper to taste.

ELECTRIC SKILLET

Dressed Trout

2 (12-oz.) fresh or frozen dressed
   trout (with head and tail)
3 Tbsp. soy sauce
2 Tbsp. dry sherry
2 Tbsp. grated gingerroot
cooking oil for deep frying
6 green onions, bias-sliced into 1 1/2 inch lengths

2 cloves garlic, minced
1 Tbsp. cooking oil
1 Tbsp. hot bean sauce
1 Tbsp. cornstarch
1 tsp. sugar
1 cup cold water

Thaw fish, if frozen. Score each fish with about eight 1/8-inch deep diagonal cuts on each side (this allows the seasonings to penetrate). For marinade, combine soy sauce, dry sherry, and gingerroot. Place fish in a shallow baking dish. Pour marinade over fish, making sure it penetrates all cuts. Let stand at room temperature for 20 minutes, turning fish over after 10 minutes. Drain fish, reserving marinade. Pat fish dry with paper towel. Pour cooking oil into a large skillet to depth of 3/4 inch; heat oil. Cook fish in hot oil 3 to 4 minutes. Turn fish and cook 3 to 4 minutes more or until fish flakes easily when tested with a fork. Drain fish on paper towel; keep warm while preparing sauce.

Sauce: In small saucepan saute onions and garlic in 1 tablespoon hot oil until tender, stir in hot bean sauce. Combine cornstarch and sugar; blend in cold water and reserve marinade. Add to mixture in saucepan. Cook and stir until thickened and bubbly. Pour sauce over fish. Serves 4.

Fish Ole'

1 lb. fish fillets
1 onion, sliced thin
2 Tbsp. olive or vegetable oil
1/2 tsp. salt
1/4 tsp. coarsely ground pepper
1 can (4 oz.) chopped green chilis, drained

10 pimento-stuffed green
   olives
1/4 cup dry white wine
1 Tbsp. lemon juice
lemon wedges

Cut fish into 5 serving pieces. Place onion in oil in 10-inch skillet. Place fish on onion; sprinkle with salt and pepper; pour over fish. Heat to boiling. Reduce heat, cover and simmer until fish flakes easily with fork, about 10 minutes. Garnish with lemon wedges.

Grandma's Special

4 fish fillets
1 tsp. salt
pepper
5 Tbsp. butter or
   margarine
1 onion, chopped

1 clove garlic
4 ripe tomatoes, peeled and
   chopped
1 Tbsp. snipped parsley
1/4 cup dry white wine
1 Tbsp. flour

Season fillets with salt and pepper. Saute onion and garlic in 3 table-spoons of butter in frying pan at 280 degrees until onion is soft. Place fillets in pan. Arrange tomatoes and parsley over fish. Add wine and 1/2 cup water. Cover tightly and simmer at 240 degrees until fish flakes easily. Remove fish and keep warm. Boil liquid until it is reduced to 1/3 its original quantity. Remove garlic. Cream together flour and remaining 2 tablespoons butter. Add mixture in frypan and cook, stirring until mixture thickens. Pour sauce over hot fish. Serves 4.

Hawaiian Style Fillets

4 large fillets (1—1/2 lbs.)
salt and pepper
2 Tbsp. lime juice
flour
3—4 Tbsp. butter
lime wedges

1/4 cup heavy cream
1 large avocado, peeled, seeded
and sliced lengthwise
1/4 cup coarsely chopped
macadamia nuts

Sprinkle fillets with salt and pepper and 1 tablespoon of the lime juice; let stand for 10 minutes. Dip fish in flour to coat all sides. Heat half the butter in an electric frying pan set at 350 degrees. Add fillets and brown about 3 minutes on one side. Turn fillets, add remaining butter, and cook until nicely browned. Remove fish to a warm serving platter and sprinkle with remaining lime juice. Add cream to the pan and bring to a rapid boil, scraping browned particles free; spoon over fish. Top with avocado slices and the macadamia nuts. Garnish with lime wedges. Serve at once.

Mouth-Watering Trout

4 trout (about 3 lbs.)
1/2—1 tsp. salt
1/2 tsp. celery salt

1/2 cup chopped onion or
1/2 tsp. onion salt

Place trout on wire rack in electric skillet. Pour water to partially cover. Sprinkle with onion, salt and celery salt. cover and cook approximately 10 minutes. Serve immediately with melted butter.

Spicy Fish Fillets

1 lb. fish fillets
5 Tbsp. butter or margarine
1/2 cup diced onion
salt and pepper to taste

1/2 cup catsup
1/3 cup lemon juice
2 tsp. Worcestershire sauce
2 tsp. prepared mustard
2 tsp. sugar

Preheat electric frying pan to 300 degrees, add 2 tablespoons butter. When melted, saute onions until brown. Remove, add remaining butter. Cut fish fillets into serving portions. Brown lightly at 360 degrees, turning carefully. Spread onions over fish. Season with salt and pepper. Combine remaining ingredients and 1/4 cup water; pour over fish. Simmer at 220 degrees about 20 minutes until fish flakes easily. Serves 4.

FISH BATTERS

All-Purpose Beer Batter

2 eggs
12 oz. beer
1 1/2 cup flour
1/4 tsp. nutmeg

1/2 tsp. baking powder
1/2 tsp. salt
1/4 tsp. pepper

Beat eggs and combine with beer. Add to dry ingredients. Mix until smooth. If batter seems too heavy, add a small amount of milk. If too thin, add a small amount of cornstarch.

Beer and Egg Batter

3 Tbsp. melted butter
1/4 cup beer
1/4 cup corn starch

1 egg
1/4 cup flour
salt

Mix beer and melted butter to beaten egg yolk. Add flour, salt, and corn starch. Beat egg whites until peaks form, but not dry. Add to mixture.

Beer Batter

2 cups flour
2 tsp. baking powder
1 tsp. salt

2 eggs
2 cups beer
1/2 cup salad oil

Coat fish with flour and then dip in smooth mixture of flour, baking powder, salt, eggs beer and oil.

Beer Batter Mixture

1 cup flour
1 can beer
1 tsp. baking powder

2 Tbsp. sugar
1 tsp. salt

Mix all above ingredients together to make a smooth batter which may be used on onions as well.

Captain Bley's Beer Batter

1 cup flour
1 egg, separated
1/4 tsp. salt

1/4 cup + 1 Tbsp. Budweiser
  beer
3 Tbsp. milk

Measure flour into a bowl. Make a well in flour; add egg yolk, Budweiser beer and salt. Stir until well blended. Gradually add milk; stir until smooth. Fold in stiffly-beaten egg white.

Easy Batter

1 egg
1/2 tsp. baking powder

1/4 tsp. salt
1 cup flour

Mix egg with baking powder, salt and flour. Thin with water.

Fish Batter

1 1/2 cup flour
1 cup milk
3 tsp. baking powder

2 eggs
1 tsp. salt

Beat eggs and stir in milk. Sift dry ingredients together. Stir into egg mixture and beat until smooth.

Fish Batter Concoction

1 cup flour
3/4 cup water
1 Tbsp. oil

1 egg, slightly beaten
1 Tbsp. salt
2 Tbsp. Parmesan cheese

Mix flour, water and salt together; add egg and mix well. Add oil and cheese; mix well. Let stand at room temperature at least one-half hour.

Fish Batter Paste

1 egg
1/2 cup flour
1/3 cup milk

1/2 tsp. salt
1/2 tsp. baking powder
2 Tbsp. oil

Mix flour, egg, milk, salt, baking powder, and oil together until mixture becomes smooth.

Pancake and Beer Batter

1 cup buttermilk pancake mix   1 tsp. salt
3/4 cup beer

Combine above ingredients and beat until smooth.

Quick Batter

biscuit mix   2 cups milk
2 eggs

Flour fish and dip fish in mixture of eggs and milk. Roll until well coated in biscuit mix. Fry in butter.

Simple Beer Batter

Mix flat beer and biscuit mix to a consistency that barely drips from a spoon.

Smelt Beer Batter

1-1/4 cup beer

1-1/4 cup flour

2 Tbsp. soft shortening

1 tsp. baking powder

1/2 tsp. soda

1 tsp. sugar

1/2 tsp. salt

Mix together all ingredients, beat until mixture becomes smooth. Dip drained smelt,other fish; or even onions in beaten egg, and roll in flour before dipping in batter.

Tasty Beer Batter

3/4 cup beer
2 eggs, separated
1-1/2 tsp. oil

3/4 cup flour
3/4 tsp. salt
1/4 tsp. garlic powder

Let beer become flat. Beat egg whites until stiff. In separate bowl, beat beer, flour, salt, oil and egg yolks, until smooth. Fold in egg whites.

The Uncola Batter

1—2 eggs
6 oz. 7-UP
2 cups pancake flour
salt and pepper

1/8 tsp. onion salt
1/8 tsp. paprika
1/8 tsp. garlic salt

Mix all ingredients together. Batter should be the consistency of regular pancake batter. If too thick, add more 7-UP. If too thin, add more pancake flour.

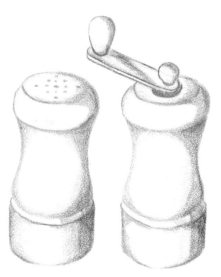

FISH SALADS

Buffet Salmon Mousse

1 lb. cooked salmon, flaked
1/4 cup cold water
2 Tbsp. sugar
1 tsp. salt
1 tsp. prepared mustard
1/2 cup vinegar
2 egg yolks, beaten

1 Tbsp. prepared horseradish
1 Tbsp. unflavored gelatin
1 cup chopped celery
1/2 cup heavy cream, whipped
olives. sliced
pimiento strips
watercress

In cold water, soften gelatin. Mix sugar, salt and mustard thoroughly. Combine with vinegar and egg yolks in double boiler. Cook until thick, stirring constantly. Remove from heat, add gelatin and stir until dissolved. Add horseradish. Chill until mixture begins to thicken. Add salmon and celery and fold in cream. Place olive slices and pimiento strips in bottom of oiled fish mold. Turn mixture into mold. Chill until firm. Unmold onto platter. Garnish with watercress.

Never-Fail Jellied Salmon Loaf

1 lb. cooked salmon
1 Tbsp. unflavored gelatin
1 cup tart salad dressing

2 Tbsp. cold water
1 cooked egg, sliced
stuffed olives

Flake salmon. Soften gelatin in cold water, dissolve over hot water and add to salad dressing. Add flaked salmon. Cover bottom of waxed papered loaf pan with slices of egg and olives. Pack salmon mixture into mold and chill until firm. Unmold and serve on crisp lettuce garnished with additional salad dressing. Serves 4—6.

Nothing-To-It Salad

2 bass fillets
1 onion, chopped fine

1/2 cup sweet pepper, chopped
1/2 cup celery, diced

Boil fillets in a cheese-cloth sack until tender. boiling water should be salted to taste. Flake the foiled bass meat and add onion, sweet pepper, and celery. Top with French dressing.

Pickled Smoked Miracle Salad

1 cup pickled smoked fish, flaked
3 hard-cooked eggs, sliced
1 cup celery, diced
basic seasoning or salt and
   pepper to taste

1/4—1/3 cup mayonnaise
2 Tbsp. onion, minced
2 Tbsp. lemon juice
2 Tbsp. parsley, minced
lemon wedges

Combine pickled fish, eggs, and celery. Blend remaining ingredients, except lemon wedges; stir into fish mixture. Serve on crisp greens and garnish with lemon wedges.

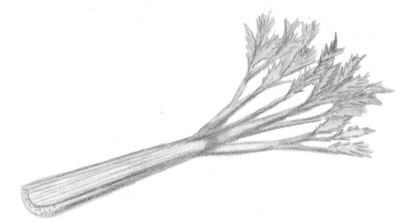

Smoked Fish Cold Salad

2 cups smoked fish, flaked
1 can (6 oz.) evaporated milk
1/8 tsp. angostura bitters
1/4 cup mayonnaise
1 Tbsp. lemon juice
2 oranges, peeled, chunked

1 red apple, diced
1 banana, sliced
1 cup celery, diced
1/4 cup blanched almonds,
   slivered
paprika

Thin mayonnaise with canned milk; add bitters. Sprinkle fish with lemon juice; add remaining ingredients and toss with mayonnaise mixture. Serve at once on lettuce. Sprinkle with paprika.

Speedy Whitefish Salad

1 lb. smoked whitefish
salad greens

1 cup wine vinegar

Marinate smoked whitefish in wine vinegar for 1 hour. Drain well. Serve on salad greens. Serves 8.

Sunday Salad

1 lb. cooked salmon, broken
    into large pieces
1 cup sliced celery
1/2 cup chopped cabbage
1/2 cup sweet pickle relish 1/2 tsp. salt

dash pepper
1 Tbsp. prepared horseradish
1 Tbsp. minced onion
1 1/2 cups salad dressing

Combine ingredients in order given. Line salad bowl with lettuce leaves, endive or romaine. Fill with salad and garnish with sliced radishes and dill pickles.

Can be served on rolls, or crackers.

Untold Salmon Salad

1 lb. cooked salmon
1/3 cup chopped sweet pickles
2/3 cup diced celery

2 hard-cooked eggs, diced
2 tsp. lemon juice
mayonnaise

Flake salmon. Combine with remaining ingredients, using enough mayonnaise to moisten. Serve on bed of lettuce.

FISH SOUPS & CHOWDERS

Bass Chowder

1 1/2 cups bass fillets
1/2 cup salt pork or bacon, diced
2 cups diced potatoes
2 cups water
3/4 cup onion, diced

2 cups half and half or
  light cream
salt and pepper to taste
butter, for flavor
1/4 cup butter
1/4 cup flour

Brown salt pork or bacon in a large pan. Add onions and saute until tender. Add potatoes and water. Cook for 10 minutes until potatoes are almost done. Add fish and cook until it flakes easily with a fork. Melt butter in a saucepan add flour and mix; incorporate into the fish stock using a wire wisk, blend well. Season with salt and pepper. Add the cream. Stir until heated thoroughly. Top each serving with a pat of butter.

Catfish Chowder

6 (1 lb.) catfish or bullheads
3 strips bacon, diced
2 Tbsp. butter
1 cup chopped celery
1/4 tsp. pepper

2 cups milk or cream
1 cup flour
1 cup chopped onion
1/4 tsp. salt
1/2 tsp. thyme

Skin and clean the fish. Boil the fish in in a large saucepan for 5 minutes in 2 quarts salted water. Drain water through a strainer or sieve into another container; this will be your fish stock. Remove the meat from bones and cut into small cubes. In another large saucepan, cook the bacon and add the celery and onion. Cook until tender then add the fish stock and the cubed fish. Let this come to a boil then cover allowing it to continue boiling. Melt butter in a small saucepan, remove from heat, add flour and mix well. Incorporate this into the fish stock. When it comes to a boil, mix vigorously with a whisk until it starts to thicken then add salt, pepper and thyme. Pour in milk and stir well. Cook over low heat until hot. Do not boil. Serves 4.

Cod Bouillabaisse

1 lb. frozen cod, cut into
  1" strips
1 Tbsp. vegetable oil
1 can (28 ozs.) whole tomatoes
1 Tbsp. snipped parsley
1/2 tsp. lemon juice
1/4 tsp. salt
1/4 tsp. dried thyme leaves
1/8 tsp. dried oregano leaves
1/8 tsp. fennel seed

1 small bay leaf
dash of cayenne pepper
2 cans (10-3/4 oz. ea.)
  condensed chicken broth
1/2 cup water
2 Tbsp. cornstarch
1 onion, chopped
1 small stalk celery, chopped
1 clove garlic, chopped fine

Saute onion and celery in oil in 3 quart saucepan over medium heat until onion is tender. Stir in tomatoes (with liquid), parsley, lemon juice, salt, thyme, oregano, fennel seed, garlic, bay leaf and cayenne pepper. Heat to boiling; reduce heat. Simmer uncovered 15 minutes. Stir in broth. Mix cold water and cornstarch; stir into broth mixture. Cook, stirring constantly, until mixture thickens and boils. Stir in cod. Simmer uncovered until cod flakes easily with fork, about 10 minutes. Serves 7.

Country Style Walleye Chowder

5 (6 lbs.) walleye	4 carrots, diced
3 onions, sliced	4 tsp. salt
3 potatoes, diced	2 tsp. parsley, chopped
1/4-1/2 lb. salt pork, diced	1/2 tsp. white pepper
1 bay leaf	2 cups boiling water
1 green pepper, diced	

Fillet, skin and cut fish into one inch chunks. Place the skin, head, bones, and tail into a cheesecloth bag and save.

Cook pork over medium heat in a Dutch oven until golden brown. Remove the pork and drain. Saute onions in the pork fat until clear. Add water and remaining ingredients and place the cheesecloth bag of fish into the water. Bring to a low boil and cook until the vegetables are tender, about 20 minutes. Add the fillet chunks and cook until flaky. Remove the bag of fish scraps and add the tomatoes. Cook for several mintues. Garnish with chopped parsley.

Creamy Fish Chowder

2 cups northern pike or other fillets, cut in 1″ pieces	2 Tbsp. instant chicken bouillon
1 qt. water	1 cup each of raw carrots, potatoes and celery, diced
1/2 cup chopped onion	1/4 tsp. each pepper and oregano
1/4 tsp. salt	1 bay leaf
2 cups medium white sauce	

Bring fish to boil in water with the bouillon and bay leaf. Simmer 20 minutes. Add vegetables and spices, simmering until tender. Make medium white sauce in a separate pan and thin the white sauce with some of the hot soup stock, then slowly stir all of the white sauce into the soup. Garnish with a little chopped parsley.

Fast-and-Easy Fish Chowder

1 lb. fish, cooked and cubed (leftover fish works well)	4—6 slices bacon, crumbled
2 cans (10 1/2 oz. ea.) condensed cream of potato soup	1 cup carrots, sliced
	1/2 cup onion, diced
	1 cup milk

Combine all ingredients in large saucepan. Heat thoroughly.

Fish Chowder-1

1 1/2 lbs. fish fillets
3/4 cup sliced onions
2 cups diced potatoes
2 cups hot water

1 cup salt pork or bacon, diced
2 cups half and half
salt and pepper to taste

Fry the salt pork until brown. Add onions and saute gently. Add potatoes and hot water and cook until the potatoes are suntil firm. Add fish fillets and cook until easily flaked with a fork. Season to taste with salt and pepper; add cream. Heat thoroughly; do not boil. Top each serving with a pat of butter.

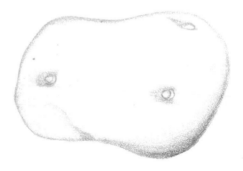

Fish Chowder-2

4 cups flaked fish
3 slices salt pork or bacon, diced
1 onion, sliced
2 Tbsp. celery, chopped
2 Tbsp. green pepper, chopped
6 potatoes, cubed

2 cups water
4 cups milk
1 Tbsp. butter
1 Tbsp. salt
1 Tbsp. thyme

Fry salt pork or bacon; add onion, celery and pepper. Saute until light brown. Parboil potatoes and brown in fat. Add potatoes, chopped fish and water; cook 10 minutes. Add milk and butter; season and serve.

Fish Chowder-3

1 lb. fish, cooked and flaked
1/4 cup green pepper, chopped
2 Tbsp. butter
1 can (10 3/4 oz.) tomato soup
1 can (14 1/2 oz.) evaporated milk

1 chicken bouillon cube,
    crushed
dash garlic powder
1/2 cup onion, chopped

Saute in butter, onion and green pepper in a saucepan until tender but not brown. Add soup, evaporated milk, bouillon cube and garlic powder. Stir in the cooked fish and heat thoroughly.

Fish Chowder-4

3 lbs. cod or haddock, cut
    in small pieces
3 cups uncooked potatoes cut
    into 1/2" cubes
1/4 lb. salt pork
2 onions, sliced
4 cups boiling water

1 3/4 cups evaporated milk
1 tsp. salt
1/8 tsp. pepper
1 Tbsp. minced parsley
1 Tbsp. butter
1 Tbsp. flour

Cut salt pork into small pieces and fry slowly in Dutch oven. Add onions and cook 5 minutes. Add potatoes, boiling water and fish. Simmer until potatoes are soft. Add milk, salt, pepper and parsley. Melt butter, add flour and blend thoroughly. Add gradually to chowder, stirring until slightly thickened. Cook 5 minutes longer.

Fish Soup

1 1/2 lbs. boneless fish,
    cut into 1/2" cubes
    (salmon, walleye, northern,
    bass, trout, etc.)
2 cups milk
3 cups water
1/2 cup celery, chopped

1 onion, sliced
3 potatoes, diced
10 peppercorns
1 1/2 tsp. salt
1 Tbsp. butter
1 Tbsp. flour

Place water and potatoes in kettle; bring to boil. Add fish, salt, peppercorns, onion and celery. Simmer until potatoes are tender. Mix flour into milk until smooth. Add flour mixture to the soup. Stir until thoroughly blended; add butter and heat until butter is melted.

Grandpa's Original Fish Soup

1/2 lb. fish fillets, cut
    into 1/2" slices
1 small cucumber
2 1/3 cups water
1 Tbsp. soy sauce
1/8 tsp. ground ginger
1/8 tsp. pepper
2 oz. uncooked vermicelli
2 cans (10 3/4 oz. ea, chicken broth)

1 can (4 1/2 oz.) tiny shrimp,
    rinsed and drained
1 cup sliced mushrooms or 1
    can (4 oz.) mushrooms,
    drained
5 cups torn spinach (about
    4 oz.)
1/4 cup sliced green onions

Cut cucumber lengthwise into halves; remove seeds. Cut each half crosswise into thin slices. Heat chicken broth, water, soy sauce, ginger and pepper to boiling in 3 quart saucepan. Stir in vermicelli. Cook uncovered until tender, about 4 minutes. Stir in cucumber, fish, shrimp and mushrooms. Heat to boiling; reduce heat. Simmer, uncovered, until fish flakes easily with fork, about 1 minute. Stir in spinach until wilted. Sprinkle each serving with sliced green onions. Serves 6

Hearty Catfish Soup

2—3 lbs. catfish, cut up
2 qt. cold water
1 sliced onion
1 stalk celery, chopped
salt and pepper to taste

1 bay leaf
parsley
1/8 tsp. thyme
1 cup milk
2 Tbsp. butter

Place ingredients except milk and butter in large kettle. Cook over low heat until meat falls apart. Add milk and butter and bring to a boil. Serve hot.

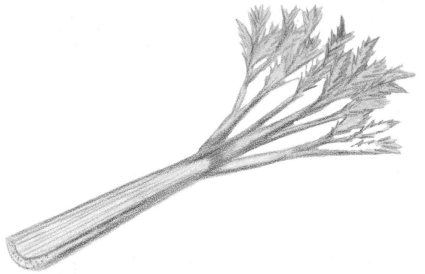

Hearty Fish Chowder

2 lbs. frozen halibut or
  haddock fillets
3 cups water
4 medium potatoes, cut into
  1/2" pieces
1 onion, chopped
1/3 cup shredded cheddar cheese

1 tomato, peeled and
  chopped
1 cup half-and-half
1 3/4 tsp. salt
1/4 tsp. pepper
1 green pepper, chopped

Heat fillets and water to boiling in Dutch oven; reduce heat. Cover and simmer just until fish flakes easily with fork, 10—15 minutes. Remove fish and broth from Dutch oven. Flake or cut fish into bite-size pieces; reserve broth.

Simmer potatoes, onion and green pepper in 1 cup of the reserved broth just until potatoes are tender, about 15 minutes. Stir in remaining broth, the halibut, tomato, half and half, salt and pepper. Heat; do not boil. Sprinkle with cheese.

Northern Chowder

1 1/2—2 lbs. northern pike
3—5 potatoes, diced
2 medium onions, diced
1 1/2 qt. milk or cream
4 Tbsp. butter
1 can celery soup

1/4 cup white wine
2 gloves garlic, minced
1/4 tsp. thyme
1/4 tsp. marjoram
1 can peas, drained
1/4—1/3 cup flour

Cover fish with salted water. Add seasonings. Simmer until fish flakes easily. Remove with a slotted spoon. Cool, remove bones and flake. Save 3 cups of fish stock. Add potatoes and onions to fish stock. Simmer until tender. Add milk or cream, butter and wine. Heat slowly. Do not boil. Add flour to desired consistency. Add soup and peas. Heat throughly at low temperature. Serves 10—12.

One More Chowder

1 1/2 lbs. cleaned fish (prefer-
  ably whitefish)
3 cups milk
2 bay leaves, crushed
1/2 tsp. dried sweet basil
4 strips bacon, diced

4 potatoes, diced
1 onion, diced
1 Tbsp. Worcestershire sauce
2 Tbsp. butter
salt and pepper

Cover fish with cold cold water in large kettle. Add bay leaves and basil. Bring to a boil and simmer 10 minutes. Drain and cool fish. Remove meat from bones. Brown the bacon and onion together. Add the potatoes and enough water to cover. Season with salt and pepper and cook until the potatoes are tender. Mash with a fork and continue cooking until the mixture is thick, stirring frequently. Add the fish and milk and heat (don't boil). Remove from heat, add butter, Worcestershire sauce and salt and pepper before serving.

Quick Chowder

2 lbs. raw fish, cut
  into cubes
6 large potatoes, diced
1 large tomato, chopped
2/3 cup butter

1 cup heavy cream
2 large onion, chopped
1 1/2 tsp. salt
1/4 tsp. pepper
1 1/2 qt. water

Place all ingredients except butter and cream in a large kettle. Heat to boiling; reduce heat, cover and simmer 25—30 minutes. Add butter and cream. Heat but do not boil. Serves 8.

Salmon Brown Rice Soup

1 lb. salmon, drained and flaked
3 slices bacon, cut into 1/2" pieces
1 onion, sliced
1 stalk celery, sliced thin
2 Tbsp. flour
4 oz. mushrooms, sliced
  (about 1-1/2 cups) or
  1 can (4 oz.) mushrooms stems and pieces, drained

1/2 tsp. dry mustard
1/4 tsp. dried rosemary leaves
2 cans (10-3/4 oz. ea.)
  chicken broth
1 cup cooked wild rice
1 cup half-and-half
parsley

Fry bacon in 3 quart saucepan until crisp. Remove bacon and drain; crumble set aside. Saute onion, celery and mushrooms in bacon fat until celery is tender. Stir in flour, mustard and rosemary. Cook over low heat, stirring constantly, until bubbly; remove from heat. Stir in chicken broth and rice. Heat to boiling; reduce heat. Cover and simmer 10 minutes. Stir in reserved bacon, salmon and half-and-half. Heat, stirring occasionally, until hot. Do not boil. Sprinkle with parsley. Serves 6.

Salmon Chowder

1 lb. cooked salmon
1 cup cooked tomatoes
1 small onion, finely sliced
2 cups water

1/4 cup flour
3 cups milk
1 1/2 tsp. salt
1/8 tsp. pepper

Flake salmon. Add tomatoes, onion and water. Simmer 20 minutes. Combine flour, milk and seasonings. Cook until thickened, stirring constantly. Add salmon mixture and serve immediately.

Savory Fish Gumbo

1 lb. fish fillets, cut into
  bite size pieces
1 green pepper, chopped
1/2 cup celery, chopped
1 can (28 oz.) tomatoes
1 can (15 1/2 oz.) okra

1 cup water
1/4 tsp. dried thyme
1 tsp. salt
1/4 cup butter
1/2 cup onion, chopped
2 cups cooked rice

Saute onion, green pepper and celery in butter over low heat until tender. Add tomatoes, okra, water, thyme and salt. Simmer for 15 minutes, stirring occasionally. Add fish and cook another 10—15 minutes, until fish flakes easily. Place 1/2 cup of rice in each soup bowl before filling with fish mixture.

Simply Super Creole Soup

1 lb. cod fillets, cut into
   1/2" slices
2 Tbsp. butter
1 can (28 ozs.) whole tomato
1/2 cup peanut butter
1/2 tsp. salt

1 package (10 oz.) frozen
   sliced okra
2 onions, sliced
2 tsp. chili powder
1 green pepper, chopped
   (about 1/2 cup)

Saute onion and chili powder in butter in 4-quart Dutch oven over medium heat until onion is tender. Stir in tomatoes (with liquid), peanut butter and salt. Break up tomatoes with fork. Heat to boiling; reduce heat. Cover and simmer 20 minutes. Rinse okra in cold water; drain. Stir okra, fish and green pepper into tomato mixture. Heat to boiling; reduce heat. Cover and simmer until fish flakes easily with fork and okra is done, about 10 minutes. Sprinkle with peanuts if desired. Serves 8.

Smoked Fish Chowder

1 1/2 lbs. smoked fish,
   flaked
1 cup cooked tomatoes
1 onion, chopped

2 cups water
3 cups milk
1/4 cup flour
1 1/2 tsp. season salt

Place smoked fish, onion tomatoes and water in a saucepan and simmer for 20 minutes. In a separate pan combine flour, milk and seasoning. Cook until thickened, stirring constantly. Mix flour-milk mixture with the fish mixture and serve immediately.

Something Different Soup

2 lbs. white fish (halibut,
  haddock, pollack, cod)
2 onions, chopped
3 cloves garlic, crushed
1/4 cup olive or vegetable oil
3 tomatoes, chopped
1 cup clam juice
6 cups water

1/2 tsp. thyme leaves
1/2 tsp. fennel seed, crushed
1/2 tsp. ground turmeric
1/8 tsp. pepper
1 bay leaf
12 slices French bread, cut
  3/4" thick
2 tsp. salt

Place bread in single layer on cookie sheet. Bake in 325 degrees oven until crisp, about 30 minutes. Saute onions and garlic in oil in Dutch oven over medium heat until onions are tender. Add tomatoes, clam juice, water, salt, thyme, fennel seed, turmeric, pepper and bay leaf. Heat to boiling; reduce heat. Cover and cook 5 minutes.

Cut fish into 1 inch pieces; add to tomato mixture. Heat to boiling; reduce heat. Cover and cook until fish flakes easily with fork.

Unbelievable Lettuce-Fish Soup

1/2 lb. walleye fillets
2 tsp. vegetable oil
1 tsp. cornstarch
1/2 tsp. salt
1/2 tsp. soy sauce
1/4 tsp. sesame oil

dash of white pepper
1/2 head lettuce
4 cups chicken broth
1 tsp. salt
1 green onion, chopped

Cut fish into 1/2 inch slices. Toss fish, vegetable oil, cornstarch, salt, soy sauce, sesame oil and white pepper in quart bowl. Cover and refrigerate 30 minutes. Remove core from lettuce; cut lettuce into 8 pieces.

Heat chicken broth to boiling in 3 quart saucepan. Add lettuce and 1 teaspoon salt; heat to boiling. Stir in fish. Heat to boiling; remove from heat. Stir in chopped green onion. Serves 5.

What's New Fish Soup

1 lb. fish fillets, cut into
   1" pieces
3 cloves garlic, mashed
1/2 cup butter
12 slices French bread
1 clove garlic, cut in half
1 1/2 cups mayonnaise or
   salad dressing

1 1/2 cups dry white wine
6 slices onion
3 slices lemon
5 sprigs parsley
1 bay leaf
1 tsp. salt
paprika

Mix mayonnaise and 3 cloves garlic; cover and refrigerate. Melt 1/4 cup of the butter in skillet. Toast 6 of the bread slices in skillet over medium heat until brown on both sides; rub one side of bread with half clove garlic. Remove from skillet; keep warm. Repeat with remaining French bread.

Place fish in single layer in skillet. Add wine, onion and lemon slices, parsley, bay leaf, salt and just enough water to cover. Heat to boiling; reduce heat. Simmer uncovered until fish flakes easily with fork, about 6 minutes. Remove fish with slotted spoon; keep warm until serving time.

Strain fish broth. Pour 1 1/2 cups of the broth into 2 quart saucepan; gradually beat in mayonnaise mixture. Cook over low heat, stirring constantly, until slightly thickened. Place 2 slices of French bread upright in each soup bowl; spoon fish between slices. Pour soup over fish; sprinkle with paprika. Serves 6.

FISH STUFFINGS

Dill Pickle Stuffing

3 cups soft bread crumbs
1/2 tsp. salt
1/8 tsp. pepper
3 Tbsp. onion, minced

1/3 cup melted butter
1/4 cup chopped dill pickle
2 Tbsp. parsley, chopped

Mix bread crumbs with seasonings and onion; add butter slowly and toss stuffing until mixed. Add dill pickle and parsley. Stuffing for 4 pound fish.

Minced Shrimp Dressing

1/2 cup boiled shrimp
1 1/2 tsp water
1 tsp. anchovy paste
1 cup soft bread crumbs

2 tsp. chopped olives
2 Tbsp. butter
1 Tbsp. grated onion
1 Tbsp. lemon juice

Heat butter, water and anchovy paste together until butter is melted. Add to bread crumbs with remaining ingredients. Good with trout. Stuffing for 3- to 4-pound fish.

Typical Bread Stuffing

2 cups soft bread crumbs
1/3 cup grated onion
1/2 cup chopped celery
1 Tbsp. lemon juice

1/2 tsp. salt
3 Tbsp. melted butter
2 Tbsp. water

Combine ingredients lightly but thoroughly. Stuffing for 3—4 pound fish.

Yummy Oyster or Clam Stuffing

1/2 cup chopped oysters
    or clams
2 cups fine cracker crumbs
2 Tbsp. butter, melted

1 tsp. salt
2 tsp. chopped pickle
2 Tbsp. lemon juice
1/2 cup water

Mix ingredients in order given, adding more water if stuffing seems dry. Oyster or clam liquid may be substituted for part of the water. Stuffing for 3—4 pound fish.

194

FISH IN A WOK

Fish Chow Mein Style

1 lb. walleye or bass fillets
1 1/2 tsp. vegetable oil
1 tsp. cornstarch
1/2 tsp. salt
1/2 tsp. light soy sauce
1/8 tsp. white pepper
1/8 tsp. sesame oil
1 lb. bok choy (about 7 stalks)
6 oz. pea pods
4 oz. mushrooms
2 green onions (with tops)

2 Tbsp. cornstarch
2 Tbsp. cold water
1/4 cup vegetable oil
1 tsp. finely chopped garlic
1 tsp. finely chop. gingerroot
2 Tbsp. vegetable oil
1 Tbsp. oyster sauce or 1 Tbsp
   dark soy sauce
1 tsp. salt
1/2 cup chicken broth

Cut fish across grain into 1/2-inch strips. Toss fish strips, 1 1/2 teaspoons vegetable oil, 1 teaspoon cornstarch, 1/2 teaspoon salt, the soy sauce, white pepper and sesame oil in glass or plastic bowl. Cover and refrigerate 30 minutes.

Separate bok choy leaves from stems. Cut leaves into 2-inch pieces; cut stems diagonally into 1/4-inch slices (do not combine leaves and stems). Remove strings from pea pods. Place pea pods in boiling water. Cover and cook 1 minute; drain. Immediately rinse under running cold water; drain. Cut mushrooms into 1/2-inch slices. Cut green onions into 2-inch pieces. Mix 2 tablespoons cornstarch and the water.

When wok is hot, add 1/4 cup vegetable oil; rotate wok to coat side. Add gingerroot and garlic; stir-fry until light brown. Add fish; stir-fry until fish turns white. Remove fish from wok.

Add 2 tablespoons vegetable oil to wok; rotate to coat side. Add bok choy stems and mushrooms; stir-fry 1 minute. Stir in bok choy leaves, oyster sauce and 1 teaspoon salt. Stir in chicken broth; heat to boiling. Stir in cornstarch mixture; cook and stir until thickened. Add fish and pea pods; stir-fry 1 minute. Garnish fish with green onions. Makes 6 servings.

Fish Hash Wonder

2 cups cooked flaked fish,
  haddock, cod or tuna
3 slices thick-sliced bacon,
  chopped
1 onion, peeled, minced
1/2 cup celery, chopped

2 cups diced cooked potatoes
1 cup cooked green peas
1/2 cup pimiento, chopped and
  drained
salt and pepper to taste
tomato catsup, for garnish

Place bacon in wok over low heat. Cook until crisp. Remove bacon. Drain on paper towel, crumble and set aside. Remove all but 2 table-spoons bacon fat and set aside. Increase heat to medium high. Add onion and chopped celery. Stir-fry until soft. Add diced potatoes. If necessary, add a little more bacon fat. Cook, stirring until lightly browned. Add peas, fish and reserved bacon. Stir-fry only until heated. Salt and pepper to taste. Place on serving plate. If desired, garnish with catsup.

Grapefruit Flounder

4 (1/2 lb.) flounder fillets
3 Tbsp. minced green onion
1 Tbsp. minced fresh ginger
salt and pepper to taste

1/2 cup dry white wine
2 Tbsp. butter
2 cups whole grapefruit
   sections, well drained

Arrange fillets in shallow baking dish. Sprinkle with onion, ginger, salt and pepper. Pour wine over fillets and dot with butter. Surround with grapefruit sections. Place on rack in wok over simmering water. Cover wok and steam for 8 to 10 minutes or until fish flakes easily when touched with fork. Serve immediately. Makes 4 servings.

Steamed Fish Surprise

1 whole fish, about 1 1/2 lbs.
   (rock cod, perch, trout, sea bass)
3 green onions
2 cloves garlic, smashed and minced

3 slices ginger root, grated
2 Tbsp. soy sauce
3 Tbsp. peanut oil

Clean and scale fish. Sprinkle 1/2 teaspoon salt on each side of fish. Cut 1 green onion in half, lengthwise and put on serving plate; place fish on top of it. Fill wok with enough water to be close to steamer plate but not touching it. Bring to boil. Place serving dish with fish on the steamer plate and cover. Steam for 15 minutes. When fish is almost cooked, grate 2 green onions and set aside. Heat oil in saucepan and saute garlic and ginger root until golden brown. Remove fish and serving dish from wok. Pour off any juices from cooked fish. Sprinkle grated onion over fish, top with hot garlic, gingerroot and soy sauce. Serve immediately.

Sweet-and-Sour Fish Fry

1 1/2 lbs. fish fillets, cut
   crosswise in 2" strips
1 cup flour, mixed with 1 tsp.
   salt, 1/2 tsp. pepper

oil for deep-frying
Sweet-and-Sour Sauce (see
   below)

Blot fish strips dry. Rub flour mixture into each strip. Pour oil in wok to a 3 inch center depth. Fry a few fish strips at a time in the hot oil until lightly browned. Pour sauce over fried fish strips and serve. Makes 4 to 6 servings.

Sweet-and-Sour Sauce:

1/3 cup soy sauce
1 Tbsp. lemon juice
1 Tbsp. cider vinegar
2 Tbsp. sugar

2 Tbsp. catsup
1 Tbsp. onion, grated
salt and pepper to taste

Combine sauce ingredients in small saucepan. Cook, stirring until well heated.

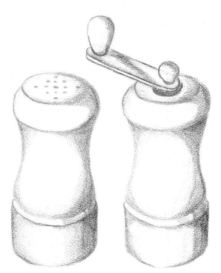

Wine Sauce Fillets

1 lb. fish fillet
  (rock cod, butter fish)
2 green onions, cut into 1" pieces
3 Tbsp. cornstarch mixed with 1/2
  cup water
2 egg whites, beaten
3/4 cup peanut oil
1 cup chicken stock

3 Tbsp. sherry
1 tsp. salt
1 Tbsp. sugar-thickening:
  1 1/2 tsp. cornstarch
    mixed with 2 Tbsp. water
2 green onions, cut into
  1" pieces

Cut fillets into 2x3 inch pieces. Cut onions, set aside. Prepare cornstarch and water in one bowl; egg whites in another. Dip fish into egg whites then into cornstarch/water mixture. Heat oil in wok until warm and immerse fish in oil for 2 minutes. In a saucepan, heat chicken stock, sherry, salt and sugar. Remove fish from oil and cook fish in sauce for 2 minutes. Add the thickening and 1 tablespoon hot oil from wok to cooking sauce. Add green onion. Heat throughly and serve immediately.

Wok Talk Fillets

4 (6 oz.) fresh fillets,	salt and pepper to taste
flounder, red snapper or trout	1/2 cup parsley, minced
2 Tbsp. oil	1/4 cup lemon juice
4 Tbsp. butter	lemon wedges, for garnish
1 glove garlic, peeled and finely minced	

Wash and dry the fish. Cut each in 1 1/2 inch pieces. Dredge in flour. Heat oil and butter. When butter melts and begins to sizzle add a few fish pieces at a time. Cook quickly over medium heat, turning until lightly browned on both sides. Remove and set aside. Add garlic to oil and butter. Stir-fry about 15 seconds. Remove wok from heat. Add fish, salt, pepper, parsley and lemon juice. Toss fish briefly in mixture. Garnish with lemon wedges. Serves 4.

FRYING

Almondine Fillets

8—12 trout fillets	4 drops hot sauce
1 1/2 cup flour	milk to cover
1 stick butter	1 tsp. white pepper
2 tsp. salt	2 Tbsp. oil

Sauce:

2 sticks butter	2 Tbsp. lemon juice
1/2 cup almonds	1 tsp. salt
2 Tbsp. Worcestershire sauce	1/4 cup parsley, chopped

Mix milk, 1 teaspoon salt, and hot sauce. Soak fish in mixture for at least 30 minutes. Mix flour, 1 teaspoon salt and white pepper together. Remove fish from milk mixture and pat dry. Coat lightly with flour mixture. Melt 1 stick butter and oil in saucepan. In large skillet pour butter mixture until 1/8 inch deep. When hot, fry fillets, turning only once and not crowding. Keep grease very hot and at right depth by adding more mixture from saucepan.

Sauce: Melt 2 sticks butter in skillet. Add almonds and lightly brown. Add lemon juice, Worcestershire sauce, salt and parsley. Mix and heat well. Just before serving, pour sauce over fillets and serve remaining sauce in sauce boat.

Amazing Fish in Tomato and Egg Sauce

1—1 1/2 lbs. fish fillets cut crosswise into 1" thick slices	1 tomato, chopped
	1 cup water
1 Tbsp. + 1 tsp. salt	2 eggs, lightly beaten
1 cup + 2 Tbsp. oil	1/4 cup scallions, chopped,
1 tsp. garlic, finely chopped	including green tops
1/3 cup onions, chopped	

Wash and pat dry fish. Sprinkle fish evenly on both sides with salt. Add all the fish to 1 cup of hot but not smoking oil. Arrange in one layer. Fry for 5—6 minutes on each side. Remove fish. In clean skillet heat 2 tablespoons oil. Drop in garlic and stir until it browns lightly. Add onions until soft. Do not burn. Add the tomato and cook for 3—4 minutes. Stir in water and salt and return fish to skillet. Pour in eggs, stirring gently into the sauce until they form soft creamy curds. Sprinkle the top with scallions and serve at once.

Bali Hai Poi

1—3 lb. fresh fish, scaled
  and dressed
cornstarch

1 1/2 quarts oil
Bali Hai Sauce (below)

Bali Hai Sauce:

3/4 cup sugar
1/2 cup cider vinegar
1/2 cup catsup
1/2 cup water
1 lemon, juiced

1 tsp. soy sauce
1/4 cup cornstarch dissolved in
1/4 cup water
1/4 cup frozen baby peas

Make 5—6 DEEP diagonal slashes on each side of fish. Shake fish so it opens up. Set aside to make sauce. Combine sugar, vinegar, catsup, water and lemon juice, cook over medium heat 3—4 minutes. Add soy sauce and dissolved cornstarch. Bring to a boil, stirring constantly. Cook until thick and clear. Add peas, then keep warm. Sprinkle both sides of fish with cornstarch. Carefully place fish into hot oil (375 degrees). Fry 7—10 minutes on both sides until brown. Remove carefully and drain well. Pour warm sauce over fish.

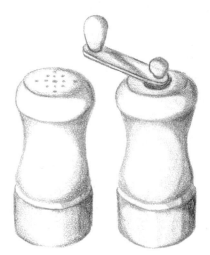

Basic Crappie Fry

1 1/2 cups pancake mix
1 tsp. salt

2 tsp. paprika
2 tsp. pepper

Scale and clean fish. Wash and dry well. Mix flour and seasoning in paper sack. Place fish in bag and shake. Remove fish and fry in hot fat 7—10 minutes on each side.

Bass 'N' Beer

6 bass fillets
2 Tbsp. flour
2 cups beer
2 tsp. salt
1 Tbsp. brown sugar
4 Tbsp. butter

1/4 tsp. pepper
paprika
2 cloves
4 Tbsp. onion, minced
1 Tbsp. lemon juice

Clean and dry fish. Sprinkle with salt, pepper, and paprika. Saute onion in butter. Add flour until brown. Gradually add beer stirring until it reaches the boiling point. Place fish in sauce and add sugar and cloves. Cover loosely and cook 30 minutes over low heat. Remove fish from sauce. Stir lemon juice into sauce then pour sauce over fish.

Beet-Fish-Hash Omelette

3/4 cup fish, cooked, flaked
3/4 cup potatoes, cooked, chopped
2 medium beets, cooked, chopped
1 Tbsp. minced onion
1 Tbsp. minced parsley

1/2 tsp. salt
1/4 tsp. paprika
1 tsp. Worcestershire sauce
3 Tbsp. cream or milk
1 1/2 Tbsp. fat

Mix first 8 ingredients and moisten with cream. Cook in fat, stirring until hot; then pat lightly into a cake and cook until well browned underneath. Fold like an omelette and serve.

Bluegill Shake

6—8 bluegills
1 1/2 cups pancake mix 1 tsp. paprika
1 tsp. salt 1 Tbsp. pepper

Scale, clean, wash and dry fish well. Combine pancake mix and seasoning in paper sack. Put fish in sack and shake until well coated. Remove fish and fry in very hot oil 7—10 minutes on each side. Remove and drain well on paper towels. Keep fish warm until served.

Bucketmouth Scramble

1 cup largemouth, cooked,
  flaked
3—5 eggs
1/4 cup milk

2 Tbsp. butter
salt and pepper to taste
chopped onions

Mix eggs with largemouth flakes. Add milk, onion, and salt and pepper. Fry in melted butter.

Celebrated Walleye

3 walleyes
2 onions, minced
3 carrots, diced
1/8 tsp. thyme
3 sprigs parsley
12 mushrooms, sauteed
  lightly in butter

24 white onions,
  steamed in butter
champagne (enough to
  cover fish)
6 pats butter, dipped in
  flour

Place onions, carrots, thyme and parsley in deep saucepan. Place walleyes on top and cover with champagne. Cover and simmer for 35 minutes, or until fish are tender. Remove fish with a holed skimmer and keep warm. Strain broth and reheat it, stirring in the flour-dipped butter pats and blending. Add mushrooms and white onions, Stirring well into the broth. When broth bubbles and vegetables are heated, pour over walleyes.

Cheesey Perch

1 lb. fillets
1/4 cup flour
1 egg, beaten
1 tsp. salt
1/8 tsp. pepper
1/4 cup fine dry bread crumbs

1/4 cup Parmesan cheese, grated
1/4 cup shortening
1 can tomato sauce (8 oz.)
1/2 tsp. sugar
1/2 tsp. basil leaves (dried,
  crushed)

Cut fish into serving size portions. Coat with flour and dip into a mixture of egg, salt and pepper, then dip into a mixture of bread crumbs and cheese. Fry fish slowly in a skillet of hot shortening until browned on one side. Turn and brown other side. Combine tomato sauce, 1/4 cup water, sugar and basil in a saucepan. Simmer 10 minutes and serve with the fish.

Corn Meal Fry

1 lb. fish fillets
2 Tbsp. all-purpose flour
1 tsp. salt

1/4 tsp. paprika
1/2 cup yellow corn meal
1/4 cup salad oil

Combine corn meal, flour, salt and paprika. Dip fish in corn meal mixture to coat. Fry fillets in hot oil until brown and fish flakes easily when tested with fork. Do not overcook.

Crispy Fish Fillets

2 lbs. fish fillets
1/2 cup Italian, Caesar or
   Russian salad dressing

salt and pepper
1 cup bread or cracker crumbs

Sprinkle fish with salt and pepper. Dip into salad dressing, then into crumbs. Fry over medium heat in small amount of hot fat until crisp and fish flakes.

Crunchy Crappies

2 lbs. crappie fillets
1 egg
2 cups butter flavored crackers,
   finely crushed

1 1/2 tsp. onion powder
2 tsp. garlic salt
1/2 cup beer
cooking oil

Sprinkle 1/2 teaspoon of a mixture of garlic salt and onion powder over fillets. Add the remaining mixture into the cracker crumbs. Beat egg into the beer. Dip fillets into the beer mixture then roll into the cracker crumb mixture until well coated. Fry fillets for about 4 minutes per side in about 1/4 inch cooking oil at 375 degrees, or until golden brown.

Deliciously Trouty

7—8 trout   1 tsp. salt
1/2—3/4 cup cracker crumbs   1/2 tsp. pepper
1/2 Tbsp. onion flakes   1/8 tsp. garlic salt
1 egg

In Separate Bowl:

3/4 cup cornflake crumbs   1 egg, beaten well

Boil trout in pan about 5 minutes. Remove and peel skin and debone. Crumble into small pieces. Add to trout the cracker crumbs, 1 egg, onion, garlic, salt and pepper. Shape into patties. Dip patties into beaten egg then roll in cornflake crumbs. Fry in hot oil until golden brown on both sides.

Delightfully Barbecued Fillets

1 lb. fish fillets
2 Tbsp. butter or margarine

1/2 cup onion, diced
salt and pepper

Barbecue Sauce:

1/2 cup catsup
1/3 cup lemon juice
1/4 cup water
2 tsp. sugar

2 tsp. Worcestershire sauce
2 tsp. prepared mustard
chopped parsley

Melt butter in frying pan. When melted, add onions and saute until golden. Add an additional 3 tablespoons butter. Cut fish into serving sized pieces and brown lightly (about 10-15 minutes), turning carefully. Spread onions over fish and season with salt and pepper. Mix barbecue sauce ingredients and pour over fish. Simmer for 20 minutes until fish flakes easily. Garnish with chopped parsley.

Down-Mexico-Way Walleye

6 walleye, cleaned
1 egg, beaten
2 Tbsp. milk
1/2 cup cornmeal
1/2 cup flour

1/4 tsp. liquid hot sauce
1 tsp. salt
1 tsp. chili powder
fat for frying
hot chili sauce

Mix egg, milk, salt, chili powder and liquid hot sauce together. Combine cornmeal and flour together. Dip fish into egg mixture then into flour mixture. Fry over medium heat about 5 minutes per side turning carefully, until fish flakes easily and are brown. Drain and serve with Hot chili sauce below.

Hot Chili Sauce:

1 cup onion, chopped
1 cup green pepper, chopped
1 clove garlic, finely chopped
1 Tbsp. shortening
salt and pepper to taste

1/8 tsp. hot sauce
1 (8 oz.) can tomato sauce
1/4 cup catsup
1 tsp. chili powder

Saute onion, green pepper and garlic in shortening until onion is tender. Add tomato sauce, catsup chili powder, hot sauce, salt and pepper. Cover and simmer 15—20 minutes. Makes 1 3/4 cups sauce.

Down-South Fillets

1 lb. fresh or frozen fillets   1/2 tsp. salt
1/2 cup flour   1/8 tsp. pepper
1/2 cup skim milk   1/2 cup cooking oil
1/4 cup corn meal

Mix flour, cornmeal, salt and pepper together. Dip fillets in milk, then roll in mixture. Fry fish in cooking oil over medium heat, until they flake easily, turning them only once.

Easy Channel Cat

4 lbs. catfish fillets
1/4 cup bacon drippings

salt & pepper to taste
juice of one lemon

Clean and wipe fillets. Season with salt and pepper. Brown fish on both sides in hot bacon drippings. Drain on paper towels. Sprinkle with lemon juice.

Easy Trout Almondine

1 1/2 lb. trout
1/4 cup butter
1 tsp. parsley, chopped fine
2 eggs, beaten
toasted almonds, shredded
1 cup salad oil

1/4 tsp. salt
1/4 tsp. white pepper
1/2 clove garlic, chopped
salt and black pepper
flour

Remove skin with sharp knife. Cut out 2 boneless fillets. Dip in eggs, and season with salt and pepper. Roll in flour. Brown fish in hot oil, turning once. Remove, sprinkle with almonds. Melt butter, add salt, white pepper, parsley and garlic. Pour over fillets.

Fancy Fillets

3 lbs. fillets
1 1/2 cups white wine
1 1/2 cups pancake mix

1 1/2 tsp. pepper
1 1/2 tsp. salt
3/4 cup butter

Marinate salt and peppered fillets in wine for 1 1/2 hours. Roll fillets in pancake mix. Carefully place fillets into hot butter. Cook until golden brown.

Fish Magic

6 fillets
2 Tbsp. flour
2 cups beer
4 Tbsp. onion, minced
4 Tbsp. butter
1 Tbsp. brown sugar

2 tsp. salt
1/4 tsp. pepper
2 cloves
1 Tbsp. lemon juice
paprika

Sprinkle fish with salt, pepper and paprika. Melt butter and saute onion. Add flour, mixing until brown. Gradually add beer, stirring to boiling point. Add fish to sauce then add sugar and cloves. Cover and cook over low heat about 30 minutes. Remove fish. Stir in lemon juice, season to taste and pour over fish.

Fish "N" Eggs

2 walleye fillets or 6
    small crappie fillets
2 eggs
seafood seasoning or imitation
    butter flavored salt

1/2 onion, sliced thin
1/4 tsp. lemon juice
1 Tbsp. milk
1 cup water

Bring water to a boil in fry pan. Cover bottom of pan with onions. Cook 5 minutes. Lay fish on top of onion slices. Season with seafood seasoner or salt. Add lemon juice. Cover and cook 8 minutes. Beat eggs and milk. Stir into fish and onions. Stir occasionally until moisture is gone.

Fish Rolls-Ups

5 fillets, flaked
1 onion, minced
3 eggs
6 slices dry bread, crumbled
1/2 cup milk
1 Tbsp. salt

1 tsp. garlic salt
1/2 tsp. pepper
1 tsp. poultry seasoning
parsley, celery or chives
    chopped

Combine fish and all ingredients together. Shape dough into rolls 2 inches long and 3/4 inch in diameter. Fry in hot fat, browning on all sides.

Football Sunday Fish

6 fish fillets
2 Tbsp. flour
4 Tbsp. butter
4 Tbsp. onion, minced
2 cups beer

2 tsp. salt
1/4 tsp. pepper
1 Tbsp. sugar
2 cloves
1 Tbsp. lemon juice

Sprinkle fillets with salt and pepper. Saute onion in butter. Add flour, stir. Gradually add beer, stirring constantly to boiling point. Place fish in sauce and add the sugar and cloves. Cover loosely, simmer over low heat 30 minutes. Remove fish to platter: add lemon juice to sauce, season to taste and pour over fish.

Forbidden Trout

4 trout, cleaned
flour
4 Tbsp. parsley, chopped

salt and pepper
1/4 cup butter

Dip trout in seasoned flour. Brown in 5 tablespoons butter until firm. Remove, and place on hot platter. To the drippings, add 3 tablespoons of butter and brown. Place parsley over the warm fish, pour the browned butter over the whole thing and serve with lemon wedges.

Fried Catfish

6 catfish, dressed
2 eggs
2 cups cornmeal

2 tsp. salt
1/4 tsp. pepper
2 Tbsp. milk

Sprinkle fish with salt and pepper. Slightly beat eggs and milk. Dip fish in egg mixture and roll in cornmeal. Fry both sides of fish in 1/8 inch hot but not smoking fat, until golden brown.

Fried Coho Steaks

1 large coho
1 cup sour cream

salt, pepper and paprika
flour

Clean fish, making sure the large silver vein against the spine is cleaned out and remove the belly fat. Season with salt, pepper and paprika. Marinate in sour cream for 45 minutes. Remove, sprinkle with flour and season again. Fry in 1/4 inch oil without crowding, turning once.

Ginger Cookie Carp

6 slices carp
2 Tbsp. sugar
1 cup onions, chopped
2 1/2 cups beer
6 gingersnaps, crushed 1 Tbsp. butter

1/2 tsp. pepper
1 Tbsp. salt
3 slices lemon
1 bay leaf

Sprinkle washed and drained fish with salt, pepper, and paprika. Arrange slices of carp over onions in deep skillet. Add beer, bay leaf, lemon and sugar. Bring to a boil. Cover loosely. Cook on low for 30 minutes. Remove fish to dish. Stir gingersnaps and butter into the liquid and cook on high heat for 2 minutes more. Season and pour over fish.

Green Grapes and Fish

2 lbs. fish fillets	1 Tbsp. lemon juice
1 1/2 tsp. salt	8 oz. (about 1-1/3 cups
1/4 tsp. pepper	seedless green grapes)
1 cup water	2 Tbsp. butter or margarine
3/4 cup dry white wine	2 Tbsp. flour
2 Tbsp. green onions, finely	1/2 cup whipping cream
chopped	2 Tbsp. butter or margarine

Sprinkle fillets with salt and pepper then fold in half. Place fish in 10 inch skillet; add water, wine, green onions, and lemon juice. Heat to boiling; reduce heat. Cover and simmer until fish flakes easily with fork, 4-5 minutes. Remove and keep warm. Add grapes to liquid in skillet; heat to boiling then reduce heat. Simmer uncovered 3 minutes. Remove grapes. Heat liquid in skillet to boiling; continue to boil until reduced to 1 cup. Reserve liquid. Heat 2 tablespoons margarine in skillet until melted; stir in flour. Cook and stir for 1 minute; remove from heat. Stir in reserved liquid and whipping cream. Bring to a boil, stirring constantly. Boil and stir 1 minute; add 2 tablespoons butter; stir until melted. Drain excess liquid from fish. Spoon sauce over fish.

Set oven to broil at 550 degrees. Broil fish 4 inches from heat just until sauce is glazed, about 3 minutes. Garnish with green grapes.

Green Pepper Fillets

1 lb. fish fillets	3 Tbsp. soy sauce
2 green peppers, cut into	1 clove garlic, chopped
1″ pieces	1/4 tsp. ground ginger
8 mushrooms, cut into halves	3 Tbsp. vegetable oil

Cut large fish into 5 serving pieces. On both sides of fish brush a mixture of soy sauce, garlic and ginger. Saute green peppers and mushrooms in vegetable oil over medium heat until vegetables are crisp and tender. Remove vegetables with slotted spoon, set aside. Fry fish in same skillet until fish flakes easily. Add sauteed vegetables; heat just until hot.

Grilled Fish Sandwiches

2 lbs. fish, dressed	3 Tbsp. flour
2 medium potatoes	1/2 tsp. salt
1 onion	1/2 tsp. pepper

Grind fish, potatoes, and onion in food grinder. Mix in dry ingredients, then form into patties. Fry in hot oil until brown.

Heavenly Trout

4 trout, cleaned
1/2 cup butter
2 Tbsp. almonds, slivered

seasoned flour
1/4 cup lemon juice
2 Tbsp. parsley, snipped

Wash and dry fish. Roll in flour. Brown 12-15 minutes in 1/4 cup butter, turning once. Place on platter, keeping warm. Melt remaining butter in skillet. Add almonds and brown. Stir in lemon juice and parsley. Pour over trout and serve.

Lemon Peppered Sunnies

10 sunfish, cleaned and
scaled
1/2 cup cornmeal
1/2 cup whole wheat flour

1 Tbsp. lemon pepper
1 egg
1/2 cup milk
cooking oil

Mix cornmeal, flour and pepper. Dip fish into egg and milk mixture then into cornmeal mixture. Fry fish in hot oil for approximately 3 minutes on each side until golden brown.

Mississippi Catfish

5 catfish fillets
1 cup cornmeal
1/4 cup bacon fat
1 cup canned milk

1/4 tsp. thyme
1/8 tsp. rosemary
salt and pepper

Sprinkle fillets with salt and pepper. Dip fillets in milk and then roll in cornmeal. Fry fish in hot bacon fat on each side for 3—5 minutes. Before turning, season each side with thyme and rosemary.

Morning Breakfast Trout

4 cleaned trout
1 cup oatmeal
1 cup milk

4 Tbsp. bacon fat
salt and pepper

Place salted and peppered trout in refrigerator over night. In the morning, cut open and debone trout. Dip in milk, roll in oatmeal, fry 4 minutes on each side in hot bacon fat.

Original Pan Fried Smelt

16—20 smelt
flour
salt, pepper and paprika

butter and shortening,
    equal amounts
lemon wedges

Clean and dry smelt. Season flour with salt, pepper, and paprika and place into a bag. Shake smelt in bag until coated well. Fry fish in hot butter and shortening until well browned.

Paddlefish Sizzle

1 1/2 lb. paddlefish steaks
    or fillets
1/4 cup corn meal
1/4 cup flour

1/2 tsp. salt
1/4 cup butter
1 Tbsp. lemon juice

Cut fish into serving sizes 3/4 inch thick. Roll fish in a mixture of flour, corn meal and salt. Brown slowly on both sides, turning carefully, about 10-15 minutes. Remove fish to warm platter. Blend the lemon juice into the hot butter drippings and pour over fish.

Pancake Fish Patties

5 lbs. fish fillets, boneless
1 cup pancake flour
1/2 medium onion chopped

1/4 medium green pepper,
    chopped
3/4 cup milk
2 eggs

Dice fish into 1/4 inch square pieces. Beat eggs, mix with fish and other ingredients in a bowl. Coat preheated griddle with oil and a large pat of butter. Make patties about 3 inch diameter and no more than 1/2 inch thick. Fry on both sides until golden brown.

Perch and White Grapes

4 perch fillets, cleaned
salt and pepper
4 Tbsp. butter

1 small can white grapes,
 seedless
juice of one lemon

Season fillets with salt and pepper and saute in half the butter until fish
are brown, 6—10 minutes. Melt butter in another pan. Saute drained
grapes, adding the lemon juice. Pour over hot fish and serve at once.

Perfect White Bass

6 bass
1 cup buttermilk
1/2 cup corn meal
1/2 cup instant mashed potatoes

1 lemon, juiced
1/2 tsp. salt
1/4 tsp. pepper
2 cups shortening

Soak fish overnight (in refrigerator) in buttermilk and lemon juice. Mix
corn meal, mashed potato flakes and salt and pepper. Roll fish in the
mixture until coated well. Fry fish in very hot oil, until brown, about 8—
10 minutes per side.

Potato Fish Puffs

4 fillets
1 egg, beaten
1 cup instant mashed potato flakes
2 eggs

1 envelope onion salad
 dressing mix
salad oil

Season fillets with salt and pepper. Combine egg and 1 tablespoon water.
Combine potato flakes and dressing mix. Dip fish into egg mixture, then
roll in potato mixture. Repeat. Brown fish in hot salad oil on one side for
4-5 minutes. Turn carefully and brown other side.

Quick Pike Patties

2 cups cooked pike
2 Tbsp. margarine
1/2 cup cracker crumbs

1/2 cup onions, chopped
1 Tbsp. lemon juice
1/8 tsp. hot sauce

Saute onions in butter. Flake pike and mix with other ingredients. Form into patties then fry in margarine until brown.

Recycled Fish Patties

2 cups cooked, flaked
   boneless, chopped fish
2 eggs
1/4 cup onion, chopped

1/4 cup water
1/4 tsp. salt
cracker or bread crumbs

Mix all ingredients together until mixture can be easily molded into patties. Fry on well-greased griddle or in a heavy frying pan until well-browned on both sides.

Remarkable Bluegills

12 bluegills
3 cups cornmeal
1/2 lb. unsalted butter

1 Tbsp. small capers
juice of 2 lemons

Roll washed bluegills in cornmeal. Fry fish on both sides in 2/3 of the butter, until crusty brown. Melt the remaining butter with lemon juice and the capers. Before serving fish remove crust; it will come off very easy along with the scales, leaving juicy white portions of fish. Pour the hot butter, lemon and capers over the fish and serve immediately.

Rocky Rock Bass

12 rock bass fillets
2 eggs
1/2 cup corn meal

1/2 cup flour
1/4 cup milk
6 bacon strips

Mix corn meal and flour together. Fry bacon in skillet. Remove when done. Dip fillets in a mixture of egg and milk, then flour mixture. Fry in hot bacon fat until golden brown.

Savory Fish Balls

1 lb. fish fillets
4 egg yolks
1 Tbsp. flour
1/2 tsp. salt

4 egg whites
1 tsp. parsley
1/4 tsp. pepper
1/8 tsp. garlic

Boil fish in water for 5—7 minutes. Drain. Mash fish with fork. Beat egg yolks until stiff. Beat egg whites until fluffy. In a large bowl, mix together yolks, parsley, flour, salt, pepper and garlic. Add fish. Then add egg whites. Make balls and fry in oil until golden brown.

Simple-and-True Trout

1—3 whole trout, cleaned
1/2 cup milk

1 tsp. salt
2 Tbsp. bacon fat

Dip trout in salted milk. Fry in bacon fat, turning each trout only once. You may quickly stir in a little lemon juice or white wine then drizzle over the trout.

Skillet Walleye

4 walleye fillets
2 Tbsp. white sauce
3/4 cup mushrooms, sliced fine
1/4 cup whipping cream
1 green onion, minced,
   including top

2 Tbsp. butter
2 Tbsp. parsley, chopped
1 cup dry white wine
1 Tbsp. chives
salt and pepper

Heat butter in skillet. Add fish, mushrooms, green onion, 1 tablespoon of parsley, salt and pepper. Pour enough wine over fish to cover them. Cover and simmer 10—15 minutes until fish flakes easily with fork. Place fish in hot, ovenproof serving dish. Bring poaching liquid to reduce it to half. Add white sauce and cream to thicken just a little. Add butter. Pour sauce over fillets and sprinkle with 1 tablespoon parsley and chives. Place under broiler until sauce is slightly browned.

Smelt, Fried or Broiled

2 doz. smelt, fresh or frozen
2 eggs, beaten
1 onion, sliced thin
1/2 cup cracker meal (omit if broiling)

1 stick butter
1 tsp. salt
1/4 tsp. pepper

Clean fish, cutting off fins. Sprinkle inside and out with salt and pepper. Dip into beaten egg, roll in cracker meal and place in refrigerator to firm breading. If broiling, omit cracker meal. To fry; Saute onions in butter. Add fish and brown over medium heat until both sides are brown. To broil; Place fish about 3 inches from heat on pre-heated broiling pan (no need to turn fish then) for about 6 minutes. Watch fish carefully so they do not char.

Snappy Trout Almondine

4 trout fillets
flour and salt
1/2 cup butter
1 Tbsp lemon juice

1/2 tsp. onion juice
1/4 cup blanched, finely
   slivered almonds

Wash and dry the fish. Sprinkle with salt and flour. Heat half the butter and onion juice in a heavy skillet and cook fish until lightly browned. Remove and place on a hot serving dish. Pour off the grease remaining in the pan and add the rest of the butter. Add the almonds and brown slowly, add lemon juice and when it foams, pour over fish.

Sour Cream Fillets

2 lbs. fillets
2 eggs, beaten
4 Tbsp. butter
1 Tbsp. curry
1 cup sour cream

1 tsp. salt
1/4 tsp. pepper
1 onion, chopped fine
bread crumbs

Cut fillets into 3—4 inch long pieces. Sprinkle with salt and pepper. Saute onion in butter. Remove onion. Add curry to eggs and beat. Dip fish into eggs, then into bread crumbs. Fry over medium heat 8—10 minutes, turning once carefully. Add onions and sour cream, cover and cook over low heat for 5 minutes more.

Super Bowl Sunday Walleye

walleyes, cleaned and dressed
1 cup flour
oil

1 tsp. salt
1/4 tsp. pepper

Roll fish in mixture of flour, salt and pepper. Place fish in hot oil and fry about 4 minutes on each side, until fish flakes easily.

Tarty Orange Trout

1 lb. trout fillets
1 onion, sliced
1/4 cup almonds, sliced
1/4 cup butter
1 tsp. salt

1/2 cup flour
1/2 tsp. paprika
1/8 tsp. pepper
2 oranges, pared and
    sectioned

Saute almonds and onion in margarine, until onion is tender; remove and keep warm. Coat fish with a mixture of flour, salt, paprika and pepper. Fry fish in same skillet over medium heat, 10 minutes, until brown, turning carefully. Top with almonds and onion; garnish with orange sections.

Toasted Almond Fillets

1 1/2 lbs. fillets
2 eggs
1/2 cup flour
4 Tbsp. butter
1 Tbsp. milk

1/2 tsp. salt
1/8 tsp. pepper
1 cup almonds, crushed
2 Tbsp. oil

Beat eggs and milk together. Mix flour with salt and pepper. Roll fillets in flour mixture, dip into egg mixture then place on crushed almonds until evenly coated on both sides. Arrange fillets in one layer on wire cake rack set over cookie sheet. Refrigerate 30 minutes. When ready to fry, melt butter and oil over medium heat. When foam begins to subside, add fish. Fry fish 5 minutes on each side turning carefully until crisp and brown.

Trout Almondine

2 lbs. trout
2 Tbsp. lemon juice
2 tsp. salt
1/8 tsp. pepper

2 Tbsp. parsley, chopped
1/2 cup flour
1/2 cup peanut oil
1/2 cup slivered almonds

Sprinkle cleaned fish with lemon juice, salt and pepper. Roll in flour, fry in hot fat until brown on both sides. Remove fish to platter, keeping warm. Fry almonds until lightly browned, add parsley and serve over fish.

Trout Crispy

1 (4—10") trout
1 tsp. paprika
1 Tbsp. salt

3 Tbsp. butter
1 tsp. pepper
3 cups crumbs

Wash trout in cold water, drain. Roll in mixture of bread crumbs, paprika, salt and pepper. Melt 3 tablespoons of butter. Add fish and cook over medium heat.

Trout Divine

4 trout, cleaned
pancake mix
salt, pepper, paprika
1/2 cup butter

1 Tbsp. almonds, slivered
1/2 cup lemon juice
2 Tbsp. parsley, chopped

Mix pancake mix, salt, pepper and paprika. Roll fish in mixture. Fry fish in melted hot butter for 12-15 minutes, turning once. Remove fish from pan, keeping them warm. Mix more butter into pan, add almonds and brown. Stir in lemon juice and parsley. Season. Pour over fish.

Trout Fantastic

4 trout
1/2 cup butter
1/2 lb. almonds, blanched,
    shredded
salt and pepper to taste

milk
flour
parsley
lemon slices

Clean trout. Remove head, tails and fins. Dip trout in milk, sprinkle with salt and pepper. Roll in flour. Melt butter with almonds in skillet then add fish. Fry until nicely browned on both sides, basting with hot butter and almonds. Spoon butter and almonds over fish. Garnish with parsley and lemon slices.

Trout Meuniere

6 trout	pepper
1/3 cup flour	2/3 cup butter
1/2 tsp. salt	lemon slices
milk	parsley, chopped
peanut oil	

Remove fins but leave heads and tails on fish. Dip in milk and drain well. Roll fish in mixture of flour, salt and pepper. Add trout to hot oil and brown well on both sides. When done, remove. Clean skillet. Melt butter until brown. Pour butter over trout. Garnish with lemon and parsley.

Trout Supreme

6 fillets	2 Tbsp. flour
2 tsp. salt	2 cups beer
1/4 tsp. pepper	1 Tbsp. brown sugar
4 Tbsp. butter	2 cloves
4 Tbsp. onion, minced	1 Tbsp. lemon juice

Sprinkle washed and dried fish with salt, pepper, and paprika. Saute onion in butter. Add flour, and stir until lightly brown. Gradually add the beer stirring until it starts to boil. Place fish in sauce then add the sugar and cloves. Cover loosely and cook about 30 minutes on low. Remove fish, stir in lemon juice. Season if need be, then pour over fish.

Trout Surprise

6 trout
6 slices bacon, chopped
1 tsp. lemon pepper
2 tsp. dried onion flakes
1 cup white wine

2 Tbsp. butter
1/2 cup seafood seasoning
1/2 cup salt
1/4 cup biscuit mix

Saute bacon, onion flakes and lemon pepper until bacon is cooked. Mix together biscuit mix, seafood seasoning and salt in a plastic bag. Shake wet trout in bag until evenly coated. Cover and cook all 6 trout together for about 8 minutes. Turn trout, add butter and wine and continue to cook for 7 minutes.

Wake-Up Crappies

8 1/2 lb. crappies
1/2 cup flour

salt and pepper
bacon grease

Clean and scale fish. Mix flour with salt and pepper, coat fish with the mixture. Fry in bacon grease until fish are deep brown and crispy.

Walleye Stand-Ups

8 walleye
1 egg white
3/4 cup heavy cream
1 onion, sliced thinly
1 cup dry white wine
1/2 tsp. salt
3 drops hot sauce

2 Tbsp. parsley, chopped
3 slices lemon
1 bay leaf
3 black peppercorns, whole
1 tsp. salt
1/4 tsp. dried tarragon leaves

Set aside 6 of the best fillets. Cut remaining 2 fillets into 1 inch pieces. Place the 2 fillets in blender with egg white, heavy cream, salt, parsley and hot sauce. Blend at high 1 minute until mixture is smooth and light green color. Place the 6 fillets, dark side up on a cutting board. Spoon about 2 tablespoons cream mixture on each fillet, spread evenly, leaving 1/2 inch edge all around. Starting at narrow end, roll fillets, fasten with toothpicks. Lightly butter skillet. To keep upright, stand fillets up straight on their more even end, so that they barely touch the side of the pan. Add wine, 1/2 cup water, onion, lemon, bay leaf, peppercorns, 1 teaspoon salt, and the tarragon. Bring to boil; cover and reduce heat. Simmer 10 minutes until center is firm, do not overcook. Place on heated platter and keep warm. Make sauce as below.

Sauce:

3 Tbsp. butter
2 Tbsp. flour
1/4 tsp. salt
1/8 tsp. paprika

3/4 cup light cream
1/2 cup fish stock
2 egg yolks
2 Tbsp. dry sherry

Melt butter in saucepan. Remove from heat, stir in flour, salt and paprika until blended. Gradually stir in cream and fish stock until mixture thickens and boils; boil 1 minute. In bowl, beat egg yolks. Add 1/3 cup hot sauce then stir back into saucepan. Add sherry. Stir over low heat until thick. Pour some sauce over fish and serve.

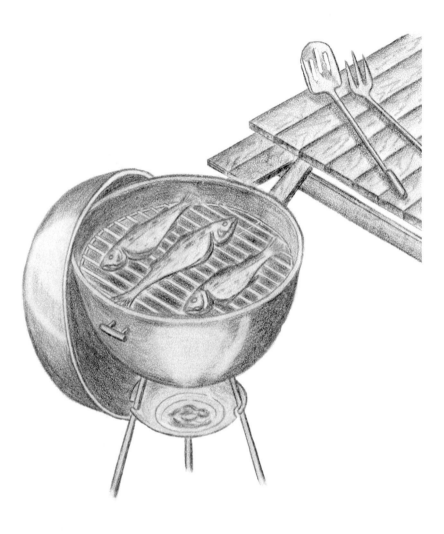

GRILLING

After-the-Catch Trout

lake trout fillets, skin on
dill weed

salt and pepper
aluminum foil

Cut fillets into serving-sized pieces and sprinkle generously with seasonings. Place fish on cold grill, skin down, then position grill about 4 inches from coals. Cover and cook for 10 minutes. Check fish for doneness by flaking with a fork; if it needs further grilling replace the cover for a few minutes more. Warning: DO NOT EAT THE SKIN, it is merely a natural container.

Always-Delicious Pike

2 lbs. pike fillets
2 Tbsp. snipped parsley
1/2 tsp. Worcestershire sauce
dash of hot pepper sauce

1/4 cup lemon juice
1 tsp. salt
1/2 cup salad oil

Combine ingredients and pour over fillets in a shallow dish. Marinate at room temperature for an hour, turning once. Drain, reserving marinade. Place fish in a well-greased broiler basket and cook until fish flakes easily with a fork, about 8 minutes. Sprinkle with paprika.

Bacon, Cheese Bass

1 fillet per person
1 slice bacon
1 onion, sliced in rings
1 Tbsp. chives, chopped
garlic powder

salt and pepper
grated cheese
2 Tbsp. butter
barbecue sauce
heavy aluminum foil

For each serving, place fillet on a piece of foil. Layer bacon, onion, chives, garlic powder, salt, pepper, grated cheese, butter and barbecue sauce if desired. Wrap in foil, poke holes on top. Cook on grill taking care not to burn fish. For a smokey flavor, unwrap fish and close lid on grill. Fish makes its own sauce.

Camper's Surprise

4 trout   3/4 lb. butter
1 package onion soup mix

Clean and wipe trout. Place each trout in separate foil. Melt butter and add dry soup. Pour mixture evenly over all four trout. Seal fish tightly and place on coals for 10—15 minutes.

Easy Grilled Pike

4 lbs. fillets   2 Tbsp. oregano
1 lb. butter   2 tsp. garlic salt
2 small cans mushrooms

Slice fillets into finger portions. Place on a square of foil. Position slices of butter, mushrooms, oregano, garlic, salt and pepper over and around fish. Place over charcoal or in oven at 350 degrees for 30 minutes.

Fishermen's Delight

2 brook trout
1/4 cup lemon juice
1/4 cup ginger ale
1 Tbsp. water
2/3 cup salad oil

2 Tbsp. grated onion
2 Tbsp. minced parsley
2 tsp. salt
1/2 tsp. pepper, celery seed

Remove heads from fish, clean, wash, and dry. Place trout in pan, combine ingredients and pour over fish. Marinate for 2 hours in refrigerator, turning fish occasionally. Place fish on oiled grill. Grill for about 5 minutes on each side, turning carefully.

Foil-Wrapped Fish

Scale and clean fish; leave whole or cut into fillets or steaks. Place fish on sheets of heavy-duty foil; brush with oil or melted butter. Sprinkle with salt, pepper and Budweiser beer. Top fish with chopped tomato or pimento and lemon slices. Bring foil up over fish and seal with a double fold; seal ends.

Briquet Covered Cooking Method: Place on grate over a medium-high fire. Bake 10 minutes on each side for 1—1 1/2 pound fish, 15 minutes on each side to 2—3 pound fish and about 20 minutes on each side for a 4—5 pound fish. Fish is done when it flakes easily. Serving with drippings from the foil package.

Grid-Iron Fillets

1 1/2 lbs. fish fillets
1/4 cup soy sauce
1/4 cup dry sherry
2 Tbsp. cooking oil

1/4 cup sesame seed, toasted
  and crushed
2 tsp. grated gingerroot

Combine soy sauce, sherry, sesame seed, oil, and gingerroot. Arrange fish in single layer in shallow dish; pour soy sauce mixture over fish. Marinate fish 15 minutes at room temperature, turning fish once. Drain, reserving marinade. Place fish in well greased wire grill basket. Grill over hot coals 8 minutes. Turn fish and brush with marinade. Grill 7—9 minutes more or until fish flakes easily when tested with a fork.

Grilled Pike

2 lbs. fresh pike fillets
1/2 cup vegetable oil
2 Tbsp. chopped parsley
1/2 tsp. Worcestershire sauce
salt

1/2 cup Budweiser beer
1/4 cup lemon juice
1 tsp. salt
dash hot pepper sauce
paprika

Cut pike into 6 portions; place in shallow dish. Combine Budweiser beer, oil, lemon juice, parsley, salt, Worcestershire sauce and hot pepper sauce; pour over fish. Marinate at room temperature 1 hour, turning once. Drain, reserving marinade. Place fish in well-greased wire broiler basket. Sprinkle with salt. Grill over medium-hot coals 5—8 minutes; baste with marinade. Turn and grill 8—10 minutes until fish flakes with a fork. Sprinkle with paprika.

Party Time Perch

2 lbs. perch fillets
1(8 oz.) can sliced pineapple
1/2 cup lemon juice

1/2 cup butter, melted
1 onion, diced

Arrange fillets in single layer in 9 x 13 inch foil pan. Drain pineapple and set aside, reserving juice. Mix pineapple juice, lemon juice and butter. Pour mixture over fillets. Cover them with onion and place foil pan in covered grill 15—20 minutes , depending on fillets thickness. Arrange coals around outer edge of grill, not directly below pan. Arrange sliced pineapple over fillets, and return to grill for 10—15 minutes more. Fish are done when easily flaked.

Quick Fish Sandwiches

1 lb. fish, cooked and flaked
1/4 cup thousand island salad dressing
2 tsp. onion, chopped

6 Tbsp. butter

6 slices Swiss cheese
12 slices bread

Combine flaked fish and dressing, spread on slices of bread. Place one slice of cheese on each and top with remaining bread. Blend butter and onion together. spread on both sides of sandwiches. Grill until brown and cheese melts.

Teriyaki Grilled Salmon

1/2 salmon (8 lbs.)
1/2 cup sugar

1 Tbsp. ground ginger
1 cup soy sauce

Mix soy sauce, sugar and ginger. Stir until sugar is dissolved. Pour into large shallow pan. Marinate salmon in soy sauce mixture for 30 minutes. Turn fish and marinate another 30 minutes.

Place fish on grill over hot coals. Grill, turning once until fish flakes easily with a fork.

MARINADES

Lomi-Lomi Salmon

3 lbs. salmon
1/2 cup chopped pimento
1 1/2 cups Budweiser beer
1/2 tsp. ground ginger
2 Tbsp. onion, grated

1/2 cup chopped green pepper
1 cup lemon or lime juice
1/2 cup soy sauce
1 clove garlic, minced

Trim salmon and remove bones. Cutting diagonally, slice salmon into thin strips 3 to 4 inches long. Spread salmon, green pepper and pimento in a thin layer in a shallow pan. Pour lemon juice and 1 cup Budweiser beer over the fish so it is completely covered. Let stand at room temperature until fish becomes a pale pink. (The fish "cooks" in the marinade). Drain fish. Rinse with cold water; drain again and lay pieces flat. Place a little of the marinated pepper and pimento at the end of each piece and roll; fasten with toothpicks. Mix soy sauce with remaining 1/2 cup Budweiser beer, ginger, garlic and onion. Use as dipping sauce with salmon.

Marinated Salmon Steaks

6 salmon steaks
3 cups Budweiser beer
1/2 cup lemon juice
1 tsp. pickling spice
1/4 tsp. whole peppercorns

3 medium onions, sliced
2 tsp. salt
1/2 cup white vinegar
1 bay leaf

Combine salmon, onions, Budweiser beer and salt in large saucepan. Bring to a boil; simmer 25 minutes. Carefully transfer salmon to a platter. Add remaining ingredients to fish stock. Bring to a boil and cook 2 minutes. Pour over fish; chill 24 hours before serving. Drain and serve cold.

Perch Kabobs

2 lbs. perch fillets, cut into
   1" squares
1 tsp. salt
1/2 tsp. crushed oregano
12 small onions
12 cherry tomatoes

1/2 cup vegetable oil
1/4 cup Budweiser beer
1/4 tsp. crushed thyme
1 clove garlic, minced
12 green pepper chunks

Combine oil, Budweiser beer, seasoning and garlic. Pour over fish; allow to marinate 2—3 hours. Parboil onions and green pepper. On 6 skewers, alternately thread fish, tomatoes, onions and green pepper.

Barbecue over medium heat 8—10 minutes, basting frequently with marinade.

Tangy Fish Marinade

1/2 cup pineapple juice
2 tsp. soy sauce
1 clove garlic (crushed)
1 tsp. brown sugar

4 Tbsp. lemon juice
1/4 tsp. pepper
1 bay leaf

Combine ingredients. Marinate fish 2 hours before cooking.

Three-Hour Marinade

2 Tbsp. lemon juice
1/4 cup olive oil

1 tsp. salt
1/8 tsp. pepper

Combine ingredients. Marinate, covered, in refrigerator 3 hours. Turn frequently.

MICROWAVING

Baked Fish Supreme

2 lbs. white fish fillets
1 tsp. salt
1/4 cup butter
1/2 cup dairy sour cream
3 green onions, thinly sliced
1 Tbsp. chopped parsley

2 grapefruit
1/4 tsp. pepper
1 can (10 oz.) cream of
asparagus, celery or mushroom
soup

Cut fish into serving size pieces and place in shallow 2 quart glass baking dish. Peel and section grapefruit over a bowl to retain juice. Drain sections. Pour juice over fish. Allow to marinate at room temperature for 10—15 minutes, discard juice. Sprinkle fish with salt and pepper. Melt butter in a glass measuring cup in microwave oven, for 30 seconds, pour over fish. Turn fish over to coat with butter. Cover with waxed paper and cook in microwave for 7—8 minutes on High. Remove from oven and baste fish with pan juices. Combine soup with sour cream, green onion and parsley. Spoon over fish. Top with grapefruit sections. Cover again with waxed paper and continue cooking 6—7 minutes at Bake, or until heated throughly.

Buttered Whitefish

1 1/4 lbs. whitefish fillets
salt and pepper

2 Tbsp. butter
paprika

Melt butter in microwave, about 15 seconds on high. Put fish into a 2 quart glass baking dish, brush with melted butter and sprinkle with salt, pepper and paprika. Cover with waxed paper. Cook in microwave for 3 minutes on high, or until fish flakes when tested with a fork.

Catfish Delight

4 skinned, dressed catfish
8 lemon slices

1/3 cup French dressing
paprika

Clean, wash and dry fish. Brush inside and out with dressing. Cut 4 of the lemon slices in half and place 2 halves in each body cavity. Place fish in a 2 quart glass baking dish. Pour remaining dressing over fish and sprinkle with paprika. Place lemon slice on top of each fish. Cover with waxed paper. Cook in microwave for 5 minutes at High, or until fish flakes easily with fork, rotate dish one half turn once. Serves 4.

Parsley and Dill Perch

8 dressed medium perch
1/2 tsp. pepper
2 Tbsp. snipped parsley

1 tsp. salt
1/4 cup finely snipped parsley
2 Tbsp. chopped fresh dill or
1 tsp. dill seed

Season fish with salt and pepper. Sprinkle 1/4 cup parsley over bottom of a buttered 1 1/2 quart glass baking dish. Arrange fish in dish and top fish with remaining parsley and dill. Cover with waxed paper. Cook in microwave oven for 4—6 minutes on high, or until fish flakes easily with fork. Transfer fish to serving platter and garnish with sprigs of parsley and dill and lemon wedges. Serves 4.

Salmon and Cucumber Sauce

4 salmon steaks, 2 lbs. each
1 cup sour cream
1 Tbsp. sugar
1 Tbsp. vinegar

1 cup cucumber, chopped
2 Tbsp. prepared horseradish
dash ground red pepper
salt to taste

For cucumber sauce, combine all ingredients but fish in a bowl and chill.

Arrange steaks in a 1 1/2 quart glass baking dish and cover with waxed paper. Cook in microwave for 4 minutes on High. Turn steaks over and rearrange. Continue cooking covered 3—4 minutes on high, or until fish flakes easily with fork. Remove from oven. Allow to stand covered 2 minutes. Serve with cucumber sauce.

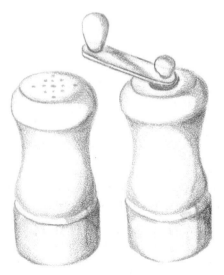

Salmon Hot Dish

1 lb. cooked salmon, flaked
1 (l0 1/4 oz.) cream of celery soup
1/2 cup celery, sliced thin
1 (17 oz.) can green peas, drained
1 cup potato chips, crumbled

4 cups noodles, cooked
1 (4 oz.) can mushroom slices, drained
1 (5 1/4 oz.) can sliced water chestnuts, drained

In deep 2 1/2 quart glass casserole combine cooked noodles, salmon, mushroom slices, celery soup, celery, water chestnuts and green peas. Heat, covered, in Microwave for 6—8 minutes, stirring occasionally. Sprinkle with potato chips just before serving.

Trout Almondine with Pineapple

6 whole boned trout (8 oz. each)
1/2 cup slivered almonds
1 Tbsp. lemon juice

2 Tbsp. butter
1/4 cup butter
6 drained pineapple slices

Place 2 tablespoons butter and almonds into a glass pie plate. Cook uncovered in microwave for 5—6 minutes at high, stir every minute until almonds are lightly toasted. Set aside.

Melt remaining butter in microwave, add lemon juice. Brush whole trout inside and out with lemon butter mixture. Arrange fish on a serving plate in a circular pattern. Shield each head with a small piece of foil. Cover with plastic wrap. Cook in microwave for 6—7 minutes on High, or until fish flakes easily with fork. Remove from oven and allow to stand covered 2 minutes. Arrange pineapple slices on toasted almonds. Cover with plastic wrap. Heat in microwave for 2 minutes on High. Garnish fish with almonds and pineapple.

Wine Poached Fish

2 1/2 lbs. fish fillets
1/4 cup onion, chopped fine
1 cup dry white wine

butter
salt and pepper

Place butter in a shallow glass baking dish. Place fish fillets in baking dish. Sprinkle with salt and pepper to taste. Sprinkle with onions and pour wine over fish. Heat, covered lightly with clear plastic, in microwave for 7—8 minutes or until fish flakes easily with a fork. Baste fish with wine and onions several times during cooking. Serves 4—6.

SAUCES FOR FISH

Basic White or Brown Sauce

2 Tbsp. butter	1 cup liquid (milk or stock)
2 Tbsp. flour	salt and pepper to taste

Melt butter in saucepan. Remove from heat. Dissolve flour in butter. Stir the liquid in gradually, smoothing out any lumps. Place saucepan over medium heat. Stir constantly, cooking until mixture boils and is thickened. Season to taste. Makes 1 cup.

Bass in Beer Sauce

3 lbs. bass, cut into serving-sized pieces	4 Tbsp. butter
2 Tbsp. flour	2 large onions, minced
1 tsp. salt	1 bottle (12 oz.) beer
1/2 tsp. black pepper	2 Tbsp. brown sugar
	1 tsp. Worcestershire sauce

Melt butter in a large frying pan. Add the chopped onion and saute until golden brown. Add the flour and cook, stirring constantly for 2 minutes. Add beer, salt, brown sugar, pepper and Worcestershire sauce. Boil, stirring constantly, until sauce thickens slightly. Add fish pieces and cook until fish flakes easily. Transfer fish carefully to serving dish. Pour beer sauce over fish and garnish with parsley sprigs.

Broiled Fish Curried Yogurt Sauce

1 cup mayonnaise	1/2 tsp. curry powder
1/2 cup yogurt	1 tsp. honey
2 tsp. parsley, minced	1 tsp. soy sauce
1 1/2 tsp. fresh dill, minced	

Mix ingredients together in order given. Broil fish until just tender. Place 1 tablespoon Curried Yogurt Sauce on top of each serving of fish. Broil one minute longer. Remove fish to serving platter. Serve remaining sauce in separate container. Makes 1 1/2 cups.

Caper Tartar Sauce

1 qt. mayonnaise
4 dill (not kosher dill) pickles,
   finely chopped

1 jar capers (2 oz.) drained
   and chopped, and an equal
   amount of chopped parsley

Mix all ingredients well. Store in refrigerator.

Cheese Sauce

2 Tbsp. butter
4 Tbsp. flour
1 1/3 cups chicken stock
4 Tbsp. tomato juice
1 tsp. soy sauce

3/4 cup cheddar cheese, grated
3 Tbsp. skim milk powder
1/3 cup water
1 Tbsp. chopped parsley

Melt butter in saucepan. Remove from heat and gradually stir in flour. Add stock to butter and flour, a little at at time, blending until smooth. Stir in tomato juice and soy sauce. Add grated cheese gradually, stirring constantly. Combine skim milk powder and water with a wire whisk. Add to sauce, mixing until smooth. Add parsley. Spoon sauce over broiled fish and broil an additional 3 minutes or until golden brown. Makes about 3 cups.

Creole Sauce

2 Tbsp. onion, chopped
1/4 cup green pepper, minced
2 Tbsp. butter
1 1/2 cups cooked tomatoes
1/4 cup sliced mushrooms

1/4 cup sliced olives
1/4 tsp. salt
pepper to taste
2 Tbsp. sherry

Cook onion and green pepper in butter until tender. Add tomatoes, mushrooms and olives and cook 2 minutes. Add seasonings and sherry. Makes about 2 cups.

For thicker sauce, blend 1 tablespoon of flour with butter and add tomatoes gradually, stirring until thickened.

Dill Sauce

3 cups sour cream
1/2 cup fresh dill weed,
   finely chopped
1/4 cup green onion, chopped

1/4 cup white wine vinegar
1/2 tsp. salt
1/4 tsp. pepper

Combine all ingredients and blend well.

Drawn Butter

In a small saucepan over low heat, melt butter until completely dissolved. Remove from heat and cool. Skim the butterfat from the top and then slowly pour into another container. Be careful not to let the fat from the bottom escape.

Note: Making Drawn Butter works best when using a tall, small diameter saucepan.

Egg Sauce for Broiled Fish

2 Tbsp. butter
4 tsp. flour
1 cup water
1/3 cup skim milk powder

salt and pepper
2 hardboiled eggs, chopped
   coarsely
1 tsp. parsley, finely chopped
1 tsp. lemon juice

Melt butter in saucepan. Remove from heat. Add flour slowly. Combine water and skim milk powder and add slowly to the above mixture, stirring constantly. Add salt and pepper to taste. Bring to boil over medium heat, stirring often until sauce is thick. Just before serving add chopped eggs, parsley and lemon juice. Serves 4—6.

Fish Curry

1 1/2 cups flaked, cooked cod
2 Tbsp. butter
1 cup Budweiser beer
1 cup light cream
dash cayenne pepper

1 onion, sliced
1 Tbsp. flour
1 Tbsp. curry powder
salt
hot cooked rice

Saute onion in butter; stir in flour. Slowly add Budweiser beer; simmer, stirring constantly, until thickened. Add fish. Mix curry powder with a little cream, stirring to form a paste. Add curry mixture to sauce; blend in remaining cream and simmer 10 minutes. Add salt and cayenne pepper to taste. Serve over hot rice.

Fish Fillets in Sweet-and-Sour Sauce

3 lbs. cod or haddock fillets
1/4 cup butter
1 1/2 cups Budweiser beer
5 peppercorns
1 tsp. Worcestershire sauce

2 large onions, chopped
2 Tbsp. flour
2 Tbsp. brown sugar
2 whole cloves
1 Tbsp. vinegar

Saute onions in butter until tender; add flour, cook 3 minutes. Add remaining ingredients except fish and vinegar; cook over low heat, stirring, until thickened. Add fish; cover and cook until fish is done. Add vinegar; cook 2 minutes.

Fish with Paprika Cream Sauce

2 lbs. trout or perch fillets
5 green onions, finely chopped
2 tomatoes, chopped
2 tsp. flour
salt and pepper
1/4 cup flour
2 tsp. salt
4 tsp. paprika
1/2 cup sour cream

2 Tbsp. vegetable oil
1 clove garlic, minced
2 Tbsp. flour
2 tsp. paprika
2 tsp. tomato pur'ee, mixed
    with 1 cup Budweiser beer
2 Tbsp. vegetable oil
1 cucumber, sliced

Heat oil in a saucepan. Saute onions; add garlic and tomatoes. Sprinkle with 2 tablespoons flour, 2 teaspoons paprika and salt and pepper to taste. Stir in tomato pur'ee-Budweiser beer mixture, cover and simmer 20 minutes. Set aside. Blend together remaining flour, salt and paprika; dredge fillets in mixture. Heat 2 tablespoons oil in skillet; brown fillets until golden. Place fillets in saucepan with tomato sauce; cover and simmer 10 minutes. Remove fillets from sauce; arrange on platter. Stir sour cream into tomato sauce; pour over fish. Garnish with cucumber.

Garden Cucumber Sauce

1 cup chopped cucumber
1/3 cup water
2 Tbsp. butter
2 Tbsp. flour
1 cup fish stock

2 tsp. lemon juice
1 tsp. grated lemon rind
1/2 tsp. grated onion
1/2 tsp. salt

Cook cucumber in water until tender. Drain. Melt butter in saucepan. Remove from heat. Stir in flour. Gradually add fish stock; bring to boil. When thick add lemon juice, rind, onion and salt. Add cooked cucumber last. Makes 2 cups.

Herb Sauced Salmon Steaks

6 (2 lb.) coho salmon steaks
1/4 cup butter
1/4 cup dry white wine
1 Tbsp. parsley, chopped

1/4 tsp. herb seasonings
1 clove garlic sliced
1 tsp. salt
lemon

Combine butter, wine, parsley, herbs and garlic; heat slowly until melted. Let stand 15 minutes. Sprinkle steaks with salt. Place fish on well greased broiler pan, brush with sauce. Broil about 3 inches from heat source, 4—6 minutes. Turn carefully, brush with sauce. Broil 4—6 minutes longer or until fish flakes easily when tested with a fork.

Baste steaks with sauce several times while broiling. Serve with lemon wedges. Serves 6.

Horseradish Sauce

1 cup yogurt
1/2 tsp. salt

1/8 tsp. cayenne
1 Tbsp. grated horseradish

Combine all ingredients in small bowl. Refrigerate, covered, until well chilled (about 1 hour). Serve as a condiment with fish. Makes about 1 cup.

Hot Curry Sauce

2 scallions, minced fine
3 Tbsp. butter
3 Tbsp. flour
1 cup milk

1 cup cream
1/2 tsp. salt
1 Tbsp. curry powder

Saute scallions in butter until soft. Add flour slowly, stirring constantly until flour is golden. Add milk and cream slowly, stirring constantly until thick. For hotter sauce, more curry powder may be added.

Old Fashioned Tartar Sauce

1 Tbsp. onion, chopped fine
1/2 cup mayonnaise

1 Tbsp. cream or milk
2 Tbsp. pickle relish

Combine all ingredients and chill.

Sauce for Baked Fish

1 cup medium white sauce
2 tsp. Worcestershire sauce
1 tsp. prepared mustard
1 Tbsp. capers

1 cup grated cheddar cheese
1 tsp. paprika
1 cup Budweiser beer

Combine white sauce, cheese, Worcestershire sauce, paprika and mustard; stir over low heat until cheese melts. Add Budweiser beer slowly while stirring; add capers. Serve hot.

Simple Caper Sauce

1/4 cup sour pickles, drained
   and chopped
2 Tbsp. capers

1 1/2 tsp. dry mustard
1 1/2 tsp. parsley, chopped
1 cup mayonnaise

Mix all ingredients. Serve with broiled, baked, or fried fish.

Slivered Almond Sauce

1/2 cup butter
1/2 cup slivered almonds
1 Tbsp. lemon juice

2 Tbsp. white cooking wine
1/4 tsp. salt
dash of black pepper

Melt butter in a small saucepan. Add almonds and saute over low heat to a delicate golden brown color. Add remaining ingredients and shake pan over heat for two minutes. Serve with fish.

Spicy Fish Sauce

1 large onion, sliced
2 cloves garlic
1 Tbsp. butter
1 1/2 cups water
1 can condensed tomato soup

1/4 cup vinegar
1 tsp. salt
2 Tbsp. sugar
2 Tbsp. mixed pickling spices,
   tied in cheesecloth bag

Saute onion and garlic in butter in large pan, until onion is soft, but not browned. Add water and bring to a boil. Add tomato soup and remaining ingredients. Simmer over low heat, stirring constantly for 5 minutes.

Alternate layers of baked fish and sauce in a covered casserole dish. Refrigerate 24 hours before serving.

Sweet-and-Sour Sauce

1/4 cup brown sugar
1/4 cup apple cider vinegar
1 can (8 oz.) unsweetened pineapple juice

1 Tbsp. cornstarch moistened
   with 2 Tbsp. water

Dissolve brown sugar in apple cider vinegar in saucepan. Add pineapple juice and bring to a boil. Add cornstarch slowly, stirring constantly until thickened. Spoon over cooked fish.

Tasty Lemon Butter

1/2 cup butter   3 Tbsp. lemon juice

Cream slightly softened butter, adding lemon juice gradually as it becomes pliable.

Unforgettable Barbecue Sauce

1/4 cup olive oil   1/2 cup lemon juice
1 tsp. paprika   1/8 tsp. cayenne pepper
1/8 tsp. pepper   2 Tbsp. onion, grated
2 Tbsp. Worcestershire sauce   1 Tbsp. sugar

Combine all ingredients in sauce pan. Stir and simmer 15 minutes. Serve
warm with cooked fish. Makes 2 1/2 cups.

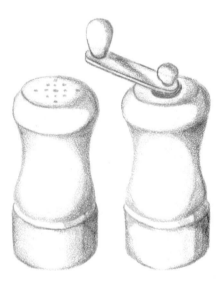

White Wine Sauce

1/2 cup onion, minced   1 Tbsp. lemon juice
3 Tbsp. butter   1/2 tsp. salt
1 cup dry white wine   1/4 tsp. white pepper
1 1/2 tsp. dark mustard

Saute onion in butter until transparent. Add remaining ingredients.
Reduce heat and simmer slowly 25 minutes. Excellent on baked fish.

INDEX

BAKING

A

B

C

D

E

F

G

H

Learn to Catch Fish in Your Home

Babe Winkelman Productions, Inc. offers you the most complete line of educational fishing tools anywhere...the tools that help you catch fish.

A. *Babe Winkelman's Facts of Fishing Video Library.* One-hour how-to video tapes featuring America's favorite gamefish. Babe couples exciting action with hard-hitting facts and detailed diagrams. Each tape covers a variety of patterns and techniques that will help you catch fish in your favorite lakes. Babe's colorful style and northwoods humor will provide entertainment for the whole family.

Walleye I Babe shows you how to catch walleyes in the weeds, suspended, in Canadian waters, in reservoirs, and a deadly approach to trophy walleyes.

Walleye II Features new approaches to walleye fishing with guest experts Bill Binkelman and Dr. Loren Hill. Plus: Great Lakes walleyes, more on weed walleyes, walleyes on pork and much more.

Largemouth Bass I Babe's favorite patterns for catching bass in cattails, bulrushes, lily pads and on the weedlines, coping with cold fronts and the fall "bonanza."

Largemouth Bass II More techniques and patterns to add to your arsenal: Bass in rice, pH, fishing the "flats," flipping in timber, dock fishing, jig and pig and learning to capitalize on the "frog run."

Smallmouth Bass I Babe explains "smaller" patterns from spring through fall on rivers and lakes.

Great Lakes Salmon and Trout I Babe will get you started with how-to and where-to-go information for catching king, chinook and pink salmon, steelhead and lake trout.

Panfish I Nearly every angler loves to catch panfish and Babe is no different. He shows you his methods for crappie, sunfish, perch, white bass and tullibee.

Northern Pike I From upper midwest waters to northern Canada's pristine lakes, Babe shows you how to catch trophy pike all season long.

B. *The Comprehensive Guide to Fishing Canada* The angler's roadmap that unlocks the mysteries of the vast Canadian Wilderness. Babe, a true expert on Canadian fishing shares his secrets and information on all major species in every province. Packed with photos and illustrations.

C. *The Comprehensive Guide to Walleye Patterns* Catching walleyes is one of Babe's specialties. His unusual methods and patterns are explained in detail. Includes valuable material never before in print. Over 150 photos and diagrams.

D. *The Comprehensive Guide to Largemouth Bass Patterns* Not just another "ho-hum" bass book. Babe uses over 150 detailed diagrams and photos to explain his "pattern system" and revolutionary approaches to bass fishing. Absolutely the last word on Largemouth Bass!

E. *Babe Winkelman's Good Fishing Audio Cassette Series* Four, one-hour tapes feature Babe answering some tough questions about catching panfish, bass, walleyes, muskies and northern pike. This one-of-a-kind item is the perfect companion! Listen and learn as Babe talks fishing...at home, in the car or even on the water.

F. *The Comprehensive Guide to Fish Locators* If you're not getting the most out of your sonar units (like most fishermen), then this course is for you. It explains sonar in explicit detail—from installation to the finest points of interpretation. Two audio tapes and a follow-along study guide.

G. *The Strictly Fish Cookbook* Not just another cookbook—this book includes illustrated "how-to's" on cleaning, filleting, storing and preparing. Babe and his wife, Charlie, have assembled a unique and tasty collection of fish recipes from around the country.

H. *Babe Winkelman's Fisherman's Favorite Polarized Sunglasses* High quality, ground and polished *GLASS* lenses that greatly reduce sun glare. Without a doubt, the best of their kind. Available in two colors: Grey for bright days, and amber for overcast and low-light conditions. Floating case and strap included.

Be a part of Babe's "Good Fishing Research Team" with official jackets, vests, rain gear, hats, polo shirts, T-shirts, patches, decals, tankards and clocks.

For complete details and ordering information, for all of Babe's products, send for a *free* catalog:

Babe Winkelman Productions, Inc.
P.O. Box 407
Brainerd, MN 56401